DATE DUE

JE 10 03			
DE 17 03			
DE 19 03			
JE 3 05			

DEMCO 38-296

Sports Quotations

Sports Quotations

*Maxims, Quips and Pronouncements
for Writers and Fans*

Edited by Andrew J. Maikovich

McFarland & Company, Inc.   Publishers
Jefferson, N.C., & London

Library of Congress Cataloging in Publication Data

Maikovich, Andrew J.
Sports quotations.

Includes index.
1. Sports — Quotations, maxims, etc. I. Title.
GV706.8.M34 1984   796   83-20005

ISBN 0-89950-100-1

Printed in the United States of America

McFarland & Company, Inc., Publishers
Box 611, Jefferson, North Carolina 28640

Contents

Foreword

A multitude of events creates each individual's perception of the world of sports. A red light spinning behind a beaten goaltender, a torn ticket laying at a racetrack and the tearful smile of a victorious underdog are but a fraction of the pictures which have captured the attention of the world. Few aspects, however, are longer remembered or enjoyed than the sound of a unique quotation.

From the beginning of organized sport, the imagination of the average sports fan has centered around the articulate athlete. You like or dislike the Muhammad Alis and Bobby Knights of the world, but you are rarely indifferent. One constant, however, is the line of fans ready to spend their time and money to watch them — and listen.

This book has been edited to provide easy access to the famous, humorous or enlightening sports quotations of the past. Sports writers will be able to find a quote before deadline by matching a present-day situation with an entry in the subject index. Sports fans can follow the changing seasons by reading quotations listed under each particular sport in session. Even the nonfan can relish the comments of other nonfans, such as H.L. Mencken and William F. Buckley.

I would like to thank the numerous individuals who helped me during my three years of research. The pleasant assistance from the employees at McClelland Library in Pueblo, Colorado, provided me with an excellent base from which to begin this project. Librarians from Colorado Springs, the University of Colorado at Boulder and the National Library of Congress were invaluable to its completion. I would also like to thank Terry Corbin, Patty Velez, Jeff Orr, Bill Hathaway, Gil Reavill, Susan Machmer, Jerry Neve, Phyllis Kaplan, Steve Kromka, Sarah Meshak, and Scott Smith for their valuable contributions.

Auto Racing

1 Champions, actors and dictators should always retire when they are on top. — *Juan Fangio, racecar driver, announcing his retirement.*

2 The crashes people remember, but drivers remember the near misses. Sometimes they aren't even apparent to the spectators, but the driver knows. When there's a near miss, when I am able to drive my way out of trouble or luck my way out, the first thing I think of is "Thank God," because I always figure that when something like that happens, I wasn't the only one responsible for avoiding it. And the second thing is that I'm sort of relieved, because I figure, "Gee, that's the one for today." — *Mario Andretti, racecar driver.*

3 During a race, it's like I become a machine and the machine becomes a man. I talk to my cars, baby them, shout at them, praise them. I feel them live and breathe in my hands. — *Cale Yarborough, racecar driver.*

4 Every car has a lot of speed in it. The trick is getting the speed out of it. — *A.J. Foyt, racecar driver.*

5 Gentlemen, start your engines. — *Tony Hulman, Indianapolis Speedway president.*

6 Getting older in racing is definitely a virtue. The older you get, the longer you're in it and the more you realize what it takes to win. You see guys 42, 45 years old racing and winning. I think my generation is going to be more alert, live longer than generations past. So you feasibly could have a race driver reach retirement age 65, and still running strong. — *Darrell Waltrip, racecar driver.*

7 He was doing exactly what he wanted to do in life, and how many men can say such a thing? Remember, nobody makes us get into these cars. Nobody puts a gun to our head and says "Drive." We do it because we like it. We do it because we love it. — *Johnny Rutherford, racecar driver, on the death of racer Art Pollard.*

8 I don't get my kicks from flirting with death. I flirt with life. It's not that I enjoy the risks, the dangers and the challenge of the race. I enjoy the life it gives me. When I finish a race, the sky looks bluer, the grass looks greener, the air feels fresher. It's so much better to be alive."—*Jackie Stewart, racecar driver.*

9 If I get wiped out and they carry me away in a box, I wouldn't expect anybody to feel sorry for me. It's something I know is a possibility, and I'm not complaining.—*Mark Donohue, racecar driver and eventual racing fatality.*

10 If it's your day, you can't do nothing wrong. —*Jimmy Bryan, Indianapolis 500 winner.*

11 If you never drove a 500-mile race, especially in really hot weather, you can't appreciate how punishing racing can be. It's like being cooped up in a blast furnace. You're in that car for four or five hours at 140 to 150 degrees, and there's nobody to help out. —*Richard Petty, racecar driver.*

12 If you win that race, or even come in second, the rest of the season is so lovely. But if you don't, it's a long hard year.—*A.J. Foyt, racecar driver on the Indianapolis 500.*

13 In company with the first lady to ever qualify at Indianapolis, gentlemen, start your engines. —*Tony Hulman, Indianapolis Speedway president, acknowledging Janet Guthrie as the first woman driver in the 500.*

14 I quit. I believe one of the marks of a successful race driver is that he can retire in one piece. —*Dan Gurney, racecar driver announcing his retirement.*

15 It's necessary to relax your muscles when you can. Relaxing your brain is fatal. —*Stirling Moss, racecar driver.*

16 It sure didn't make me the million dollars people said it would, but it sure made my ex-wife happy.—*Bobby Unser, racecar driver, on winning the Indianapolis 500.*

17 It's called being a hard charger. And there's only one other type of driver, and that's an also ran. —*Cale Yarborough, racecar driver, on his style of driving.*

18 It used to be that when you blew an engine, for example, you had time to pop the clutch, but now you're into a wall, backward, before you realize what happened. I don't know whether we need a cutback in engine sizes or higher minimum weights, but something's got to be done. —*Mario Andretti, racecar driver, in 1970.*

19 A man must want money awful bad to drive there. — *Richard Petty, racecar driver, on driving at Indianaapolis.*

20 The more money you have, the faster you go. — *A.J. Watson, car designer, on the importance of money in auto racing.*

21 My biggest concern during a race is being bored. The biggest thing I have to combat is falling asleep while going around and around. All drivers have little games they play to keep alert. I try to pick out landmarks — sometimes people in the crowd — and look at them every time around. I've startled more than a few of my friends by waving as I go through a turn. — *Mario Andretti, racecar driver.*

22 No one wants to quit when he's losing and no one wants to quit when he's winning. — *Richard Petty, racecar driver.*

23 On the day of the race, a lot of people want you to sign something just before you get in the car so that they can say they got your last autograph. — *A.J. Foyt, racecar driver.*

24 That's what everybody works to find — the unfair advantage. Something in your car that nobody else has. — *Mark Donohue, racecar driver, on the new design of his car.*

25 There's no question that motor racing is a very sexual sport. There's no doubt about it. I must say that after a long race I feel particularly sexy. — *Graham Hill, racecar driver.*

26 The thrill is watching human beings weave through murderous traffic at 150 miles per hour, with their lives in their sweaty hands. But if a man is hurt, everybody feels it, everybody hurts. — *Les Richter, former football linebacker.*

27 To achieve anything in this game, you must be prepared to dabble on the boundary of disaster. — *Stirling Moss, racecar driver.*

28 To drive a racing car, you must be conservative. You cannot be a radical, someone who's given to spontaneity or enthusiasms. — *Jackie Stewart, racecar driver.*

29 To win a race in the slowest possible time. — *Jack Brabham, racecar driver, on his racing strategy.*

30 When speed gets in the blood, one must drive to live. — *Rudolf Caracciola, racecar driver.*

31 When you are racing, there isn't time to worry about the dangers. — *Jim Clark, racecar driver.*

32 When you're driving hard out on the limit and the true love of speed comes over you, you don't want to slow up. It's always the same: The faster you go, the less you care about being able to stop — ever. — *Sam Posey, racecar driver.*

33 You don't ever drive 100 percent. You drive 105 percent ... But if you drive 115 percent, you're going to crash. Unfortunately, when you're young you do have to go through the experience of going over the limit to find out where it is. That's the reason a car owner hates to get a rookie. — *Bobby Unser, racecar driver.*

34 You get more than one of them things and you call them Loti. — *Parnelli Jones, racecar driver, on the Lotus race car.*

35 You gotta like a guy who'll go into the 21 Club and order butterbeans and cornbread. — *Buddy Baker, racecar driver, on Richard Petty.*

36 You just have to treat death like any other part of life. — *Tom Sneva, racecar driver, on the risks of racing.*

37 You may drive the freeways daily at top speeds with confidence and skill. But that doesn't qualify you as a race driver. Put an ordinary driver in an Indy-type racecar and he'd probably crash before he got out of the pit area. — *Al Unser, racecar driver.*

Baseball

38 Ain't no man can avoid being born average, but there ain't no man got to be common. — *Leroy (Satchel) Paige, Hall of Fame pitcher.*

39 All I can tell them is to pick a good one and sock it. I get back to the dugout and they ask me what I hit and I tell them I don't know except it looked good. — *George Herman (Babe) Ruth, New York Yankees outfielder.*

40 All the fat guys watch me and say to their wives, "See, there's a fat guy doing okay. Bring me another beer." — *Mickey Lolich, Detroit Tigers pitcher.*

41 An ardent supporter of the hometown team should go to a game prepared to take offense, no matter what happens. — *Robert Benchley, writer.*

42   The Angels are the first team I've ever been on where I feel I belong. They're all nuts, too. *— Jimmy Piersall, Los Angeles Angels outfielder, on his teammates.*

43   Another club can be beating you for six innings but for some reason the good ball clubs get tough and win them in the last three. *— Billy Martin, Texas Rangers manager.*

44   Anxiety is the edge I have on the pitcher and the catcher. I know that when I'm on base, they're filled with anxiety, and that gives me an edge. *— Lou Brock, St. Louis Cardinals outfielder, on stealing bases.*

45   Any ballplayer that don't sign autographs for little kids ain't American. He's a communist. *— Rogers Hornsby, St. Louis Cardinals infielder.*

46   Any manager who can't get along with a .400 hitter is crazy. *— Joe McCarthy, former baseball manager.*

47   Anyone is unsung who does not play in New York City. *— Bob Stevens, San Francisco Chronicle reporter.*

48   Anyone who rolls over and plays dead consigns himself to last place. *— Birdie Tebbetts, Cincinnati Reds manager, after viewing two knockdown pitches.*

49   Anyone who tells himself he can win a pennant with an expansion team is just spitting into a gale. *— Roy Hartsfield, Toronto Blue Jays manager.*

50   As for newspapers, a guy from the *Trenton Journal* gets as much time with me as a guy from the *Philadelphia Inquirer.* Why? Well, I know what it is like to be the guy from the *Trenton Journal. — Frank Lucchesi, Philadelphia Phillies manager.*

51   As long as some of the guys they hire today won't run 90 feet. *— Minnie Minoso, veteran baseball player, on how much longer he would play.*

52   At my age, I'm just happy to be named the greatest living anything. *— Joe DiMaggio, former New York Yankees outfielder, on being named baseball's greatest living player at age 66.*

53   Avoid fried meats, which angry up the blood. *— Leroy (Satchel) Paige, Hall of Fame pitcher, on how to stay young.*

54   Babe Ruth ate and he slept around and he played baseball. Those were the three things he did in life. *— Herb Mitchelson, former sportswriter.*

55   A ballplayer is under contract for his ability on the field, not as a human being. *— Alex Johnson, California Angels outfielder.*

56 A ballplayer's got to be kept hungry to become a big-leaguer. That's why no boy from a rich family ever made the big leagues. — *Joe DiMaggio, New York Yankees outfielder.*

57 The ballplayer who loses his head, who can't keep his cool, is worse than no ballplayer at all. — *Lou Gehrig, New York Yankees outfielder.*

58 The balls aren't the same balls, the bats aren't the same length and it's further between bases. — *Reggie Jackson, Oakland A's outfielder, on playoff pressure.*

59 A baseball fan has the digestive apparatus of a billy goat. He can, and does, devour any set of diamond statistics with insatiable appetite and then nuzzles hungrily for more. — *Arthur Daley, writer.*

60 Baseball gives every American boy a chance to excel, not just be as good as someone else but to be better than someone else. — *Ted Williams, Boston Red Sox outfielder.*

61 Baseball gives you every chance to be great. Then it puts every pressure on you to prove that you haven't got what it takes. It never takes away the chance, and it never eases up on the pressure. — *Joe Garagiola, television announcer.*

62 (Baseball) has kept faith with the public, maintaining its old admission price for nearly 30 years while other forms of entertainment have doubled and tripled in price. And it will probably never change. — *Connie Mack, baseball manager in 1931.*

63 (Baseball is) a hitter's game. They have pitchers because somebody has to go out there and throw the ball up to the plate. — *Clay Carroll, Cincinnati Reds pitcher.*

64 Baseball is almost the orderly thing in a very unorderly world. If you get three strikes, even the best lawyer in the world can't get you off. — *Bill Veeck, Chicago White Sox owner.*

65 Baseball is a simple game. If you have good players, and if you keep them in the right frame of mind, then the manager is a success. The players make the manager; it's never the other way. — *Sparky Anderson, Cincinnati Reds manager.*

66 Baseball is as much a part of America as the freedoms we cherish and the liberties we defend. If one understands baseball, he understands America. — *Bob Howsam, Cincinnati Reds general manager.*

67 Baseball is a tremendous business for men with big egos. But ego can only take you so far. After that, it has to be a good business proposition. — *Brad Corbett, former Texas Rangers owner on why he sold the team.*

68 Baseball is both the greatest and worst thing that ever happened to me. Not because people asked too much of me, but because I asked too much of myself. As it turned out, my talent was a curse. The curse was the way I handled it and didn't handle it. — *Sam McDowell, former San Francisco Giants pitcher.*

69 Baseball is dull only to those with dull minds. — *Red Smith, New York Times writer.*

70 Baseball isn't a business, it's more like a disease. — *Walter O'Malley, Los Angeles Dodgers owner.*

71 Baseball is something more than a game to an American boy; it is his training field for life work. Destroy his faith in its squareness and honesty and you have destroyed something more; you have planted suspicion of all things in his heart. — *James Landis, commissioner of baseball.*

72 Baseball is the only field of endeavor where a man can succeed three times out of ten and be considered a good performer. — *Ted Williams, former Boston Red Sox outfielder.*

73 Baseball is too much of a sport to be a business and too much of a business to be a sport. — *Philip Wrigley, Chicago Cubs owner.*

74 A baseball manager is a necessary evil. — *Sparky Anderson, Cincinnati Reds manager.*

75 Baseball, to me, is still the national pastime because it is a summer game. I feel that almost all Americans are summer people, that summer is what they think of when they think of their childhood. I think it stirs up an incredible emotion within people. — *Steve Busby, Kansas City Royals pitcher.*

76 The beauty and joy of baseball is not having to explain it. — *Chuck Shriver, Chicago Cubs publicist.*

77 Before you draft a kid, you got to know how bad he wants to play. So you don't tell him he's going to Hollywood. You tell him about the 3 a.m. bus rides, the greasy-spoon food and locker rooms so filthy you suit up at the hotel. If he understands that and still wants to play, he's a prospect. — *Gary Johnson, Chicago White Sox scout.*

78 Believe what you like; no manager ever resigns. — *Bucky Harris, Detroit Tigers manager.*

79 Bench me or trade me. — *Chico Ruiz, California Angels.*

80 The best thing about baseball is that you can do something about yesterday tomorrow. — *Manny Trillo, Philadelphia Phillies infielder.*

81 Best thing wrong with Jack Fisher is nothing. — *Casey Stengel, New York Mets manager, on his premier pitcher.*

82 Better make it six. I can't eat eight. — *Dan Osinski, Milwaukee Braves pitcher, when asked if he wanted his pizza in six or eight pieces.*

83 The bigger the guy, the less he argues. You never heard a word out of Stan Musial or Willie Mays or Roberto Clementi. They never tried to make you look bad. — *Tom Gorman, umpire, on umpire baiters.*

84 The biggest thing in managing a major league team is to establish some sort of authority without making it smothering discipline. — *Ken Aspromonte, Cleveland Indians manager.*

85 The big trouble is not really who isn't in the Hall of Fame, but who is. It was established for a select few. — *Rogers Hornsby, former St. Louis Cardinals infielder on certain players not being inducted into the Hall of Fame.*

86 Blending a team is like blending a drink. You have to find just the right mix of youthful spirits and aged whiskey. — *Al Campanis, Los Angeles Dodgers general manager.*

87 Branch Rickey said there were five ingredients that make up a ballplayer. I know you've heard them before — run, field, throw, hit and hit with power. If you have three of them, you can play; four, you excel; and all five, you're a superstar. — *Gene Mauch, Montreal Expos manager.*

88 Building a ballclub is an art, not a science. Our first instinct is to be aggressive. Go for what you need first, then worry about consequences, because there are no worse consequences than losing. — *Gene Michael, New York Yankees general manager.*

89 Calling a game with cold dispassion is a cinch. You sit on your can, reporting grounders and two-base hits lackadaisically. You've got no responsibilities. But rooting is tough. It requires creativeness. It also fulfills your function, which is to shill. You are the arm of the home club who is there to make the listener happy. — *Bob Prince, former Pittsburgh Pirates announcer.*

90 Can't anyone here play this game? — *Casey Stengel, New York Mets manager.*

91 Catching a fly ball is a pleasure but knowing what to do with it after you catch it is a business. — *Tommy Henrich, New York Yankees outfielder.*

92 The Chicago Cubs fans are the greatest fans in baseball. They've got to be. — *Herman Franks, Chicago Cubs manager.*

93 Close don't count in baseball. Close only counts in horseshoes and grenades. — *Frank Robinson, Baltimore Orioles coach.*

94 The coldest winter I ever spent was a summer in San Francisco. — *Charley Dressen, former San Francisco Giants manager.*

95 The difference is, it used to be you got paid after you did it. Now you get paid before. — *Rick Waits, Cleveland Indians pitcher, on baseball salaries.*

96 DiMaggio seldom showed emotion. One day, after striking out, he came into the dugout and kicked the ball bag. We all went, "Ooh". It hurt. He sat down and the sweat popped out on his forehead and he clenched his fists without ever saying a word. Everybody wanted to howl. But this was the god. You don't laugh at gods. — *Jerry Coleman, San Diego Padres announcer, on former teammate Joe DiMaggio.*

97 Don't look back, something might be gaining on you. — *Leroy (Satchel) Paige, Hall of Fame pitcher, on how to stay young.*

98 Everybody judges players different. I judge a player by what he does for his ball club and not by what he does for himself. I think the name of the game is self-sacrifice. — *Billy Martin, Minnesota Twins manager.*

99 Everybody recognizes that nobody won. — *Donald Grant, New York Mets chairman, on the 1972 player strike.*

100 Everybody thinks of baseball as a sacred cow. When you have the nerve to challenge it, people look down their noses at you. There are a lot of things wrong with a lot of industries ... baseball is one of them. — *Curt Flood, St. Louis Cardinals outfielder.*

101 Every boy likes baseball, and if he doesn't he's not a boy. — *Zane Grey, writer.*

102 Every club's the same. You've got two, maybe three guys who do their job and never complain, never say a word. Then you've got about 14 guys who might mumble, but they're mild, and easy to handle. It's the other six or seven guys. Every time they're told to do something, the first thing they do is ask, "Why?" They always want to know, "Why?" — *Lefty Phillips, California Angels manager, on modern ballplayers.*

103 Every golfer must learn to hook and slice when he's in trouble. When a hitter is in trouble, he should hit to the opposite field to get back into the groove, to stop jerking his head and going back on his heels when he swings. Once he's back in that groove, then he should go back to pulling. —*Harry Walker, Houston Astros manager.*

104 Every great hitter works on the theory that the pitcher is more afraid of him than he is of the pitcher. — *Ty Cobb, Detroit Tigers infielder.*

105 Every player should be accorded the privilege of at least one season with the Chicago Cubs. That's baseball as it should be played—in God's own sunshine. And that's really living. —*Alvin Dark, Chicago Cubs infielder.*

106 A faint heart is one of the big causes of sore arms. —*Frank Foreman, Baltimore Orioles pitcher.*

107 Families go to ballparks and that is why baseball is still our national game. —*Bill Shea, New York Mets executive.*

108 The fan is the one who suffers. He cheers a guy to a .350 season, then watches that player sign with another team. When you destroy fan loyalties, you destroy everything. —*Frank Robinson, Baltimore Orioles coach, on free agents.*

109 Fans want the player to be not what he inherently is but what they think he ought to be. — *James Brosnan, writer and former pitcher.*

110 First guy in checks the dugout for alligators. — *Wayne Causey, Kansas City A's shortstop, on owner Charley Finley's promotional animals.*

111 The first principle of contract negotiation is don't remind them of what you did in the past; tell them what you're going to do in the future. —*Stan Musial, St. Louis Cardinals infielder.*

112 First the players want a hamburger, and the owners gave them a hamburger. Then they wanted a filet mignon, and they gave them a filet mignon. Then they wanted the whole damn cow, and now that they got the cow they want a pasture to put him in. You just can't satisfy them, and I have no sympathy for any of them. —*Rip Sewell, former Pittsburgh Pirates pitcher, on modern day players.*

113 The first thing a manager learns is to stay on the bench. —*Mike Higgins, Boston Red Sox manager.*

114 Freddie Fitzsimmons is my man. He once hit me in the on-deck circle. —*Billy Herman, Boston Red Sox manager, on the best brush-back pitcher in baseball.*

115 Friendships are forgotten when the game begins. —*Alvin Dark, Kansas City A's manager.*

116 Funny, but there is less pressure being three or four games behind in a pennant race than three or four ahead. Last year, we kept looking back over our shoulder. — *Ron Santo, Chicago Cubs infielder.*

117 The game has to be fun if you're going to be any good at all. — *Don Zimmer, San Diego Padres manager.*

118 Gentlemen, he was out ... because I said he was out. — *Bill Klem, umpire, after viewing a photo which showed he missed a call.*

119 Get 30 games over .500 and you can break even the rest of the way. — *Ralph Houk, Detroit Tigers manager, on how to win a pennant.*

120 The Giants is dead. — *Charley Dressen, Brooklyn Dodgers manager.*

121 Gods do not answer letters. — *John Updike, writer, explaining Ted Williams' failure to tip his hat to acknowledge applause for his final home run.*

122 Good pitching always stops good hitting and vice versa. — *Bob Veale, Pittsburgh Pirates pitcher.*

123 Go very light on the vices, such as carrying on in society. The social ramble ain't restful. — *Leroy (Satchel) Paige, Hall of Fame pitcher, on how to stay young.*

124 Grading hitters is about like making out report cards. You can rate just about all hitters in baseball on a scale from A to F. There aren't many A's around. And the guys who get A-plusses, well, they're just plain rare. — *Lefty Phillips, California Angels manager.*

125 Grandmother was a pretty good hitter. — *Early Wynn, Chicago White Sox pitcher, asked if he would really brush-back his grandmother.*

126 Grantland Rice, the great sports writer once said, "It's not whether you win or lose, it's how you play the game." Well, Grantland Rice can go to hell as far as I'm concerned. — *Gene Autry, California Angels owner, on criticism of his free agent purchases.*

127 The great American game should be an unrelenting war of nerves. — *Ty Cobb, Detroit Tigers infielder.*

128 A great ballplayer is a player who will take a chance. — *Branch Rickey, former baseball owner.*

129 A great catch is like watching girls go by — the last one you see is always the prettiest. — *Bob Gibson, St. Louis Cardinals pitcher, on an excellent catch by his centerfielder.*

130 The greatest untapped reservoir of raw material in the history of our game is the black race. — *Branch Rickey, Brooklyn Dodgers owner, on why he signed Jackie Robinson.*

131 The great thing about baseball is that there's a crisis every day. — *Gabe Paul, baseball executive.*

132 Guys in baseball are crazy. They don't understand the consequences of hitting a man with a ball. They don't know the pain and discomfort and downright danger to his life. — *Willie Davis, Los Angeles Dodgers outfielder.*

133 A guy who throws what he intends to throw — that's the definition of a good pitcher. — *Sandy Koufax, Los Angeles Dodgers pitcher.*

134 He can't hit, he can't run, he can't throw — all he can do is beat you. — *Leo Durocher, Brooklyn Dodgers infielder, on Eddie Stanky.*

135 A heck of a lot better than being the smallest player in the minors. — *Fred Patek, Kansas City Royals shortstop, on how it feels to be the smallest player in the majors.*

136 He's a legend in his own mind. — *Greg Gross, Philadelphia Phillies outfielder, on shortstop Larry Bowa.*

137 He's the first defensive catcher I've had who can throw but can't catch. — *Casey Stengel, New York Mets manager, on Chris Cannizarro.*

138 He was the best I ever had, with the possible exception of Mays. At that he was even faster than Willie. — *Leo Durocher, former New York Giants manager, on outfielder Pete Reiser.*

139 His head was full of larceny, but his feet were honest. — *Bugs Baer, writer, when Ping Brodie was caught stealing.*

140 Hitting a baseball is the hardest thing to do in all sport. Think about it: You've got a round ball, a round bat, and the object is to hit it square. — *Pete Rose, Cincinnati Reds outfielder.*

141 Hitting is 50 percent above the shoulders. — *Ted Williams, Washington Senators manager.*

142 Holy cow. — *Harry Caray, St. Louis Cardinals announcer.*

143 Homers are the root of all evil. You hit a couple and every time up you're looking to hit the ball out. First thing you know, you're in a slump. — *Curt Blefary, Baltimore Orioles outfielder.*

144 Home run hitters drive Cadillacs; singles hitters drive Fords. — *Ralph Kiner, Pittsburgh Pirates outfielder.*

145 How 'bout that, sports fans? — *Mel Allen, announcer.*

146 I became a good pitcher when I stopped trying to make them miss the ball and started trying to make them hit it. — *Sandy Koufax, Los Angeles Dodgers pitcher.*

147 I believe salaries are at their peak, not just in baseball, but in all sports.
It's quite possible some owners will trade away, or even drop entirely, players who expect $200,000 salaries. There's a superstar born every year.... But still there is no way clubs can continue to increase salaries to the level some players are talking about. — *Peter O'Malley, Los Angeles Dodgers president in 1971.*

148 I blew it the way I saw it. — *Ralph Deleonardis, Pacific Coast League umpire, questioned about missing a call.*

149 I cannot agree with critics who claim there is too much stress put on the little leagues. To me, that is so much hokum. Boys must have the spirit of competition in some way and there is none better than baseball. — *Joe Cronin, American League president.*

150 I can't believe that Babe Ruth was a better player than Willie Mays.
Ruth is probably to baseball what Arnold Palmer is to golf. He got the game moving. But I can't believe he could run as well as Mays, and I can't believe he was any better an outfielder. — *Sandy Koufax, former Los Angeles Dodgers pitcher.*

151 I can't say for sure, but a couple of times after hitting against him I noticed my bat was warped. — *Jim Gentile, Baltimore Orioles outfielder, on whether a pitcher was throwing a spitball.*

152 I can't tell how good a team really is until I see them playing under pressure. — *Billy Martin, New York Yankees manager.*

153 I could see the fear in his eyes. — *Gene Mauch, former Philadelphia Phillies manager, asked why he didn't use his bullpen ace very often during the 1964 stretch run.*

154 I'd change policy, bring back natural grass and nickel beer. Baseball is the belly-button of our society. Straighten out baseball, and you'll straighten out the rest of the world. — *Bill Lee, Boston Red Sox pitcher, on how he would change baseball.*

155 The idea is to break as soon as the pitcher begins his motion — all you need to see is the guy twitch his wrist, and you take off. Usually, the pitcher will see you and panic. Eight out of 10 times, he'll do something wrong—rush his delivery and put the ball in the wrong place, throw the wrong pitch.... You're counting on the fact that the pitcher will panic. —*Billy Martin, Oakland A's manager, on the art of stealing home.*

156 I did not mean to holler so loud when he stole them two bases yesterday, but I just could not help myself. I were so proud he were black.... I want my race to hit home all the time. —*Langston Hughes, writer, on Jackie Robinson.*

157 I don't care who wins as long as it's the Cubs. —*Bert Wilson, Chicago Cubs announcer, on shilling for his club.*

158 I don't get mad at the writers. I used to, but I found out that most of the things they say, critical or not, are true. —*Mike Vail, New York Mets outfielder.*

159 I don't have any problems—just concerns. —*Eddie Stanky, St. Louis Cardinals manager.*

160 I don't know if he throws a spitball, but he sure spits on the ball. —*Casey Stengel, New York Yankees manager, on an opposing pitcher.*

161 I don't know if I'm mature enough or secure enough to not make as much as Dave Winfield. —*Reggie Jackson, New York Yankees outfielder, after Dave Winfield signed a multi-million dollar contract.*

162 I don't like to sound egotistical, but every time I stepped up to the plate with a bat in my hands, I couldn't help but feel sorry for the pitcher. —*Rogers Hornsby, St. Louis Cardinals infielder.*

163 I don't need a chest protector. I need a bra. —*Gus Triandos, former Baltimore Orioles catcher, at an Old-Timers game.*

164 I'd rather be an attendant in a gas station. You wipe a windshield and they say, "Thank you". Nobody ever says thank you to the commissioner of baseball. —*Buzzie Bavasi, San Diego Padres president, on being the commissioner of baseball.*

165 I'd rather be lucky than good. —*Lefty Gomez, former New York Yankees pitcher.*

166 I exploit the greed of all hitters. —*Lew Burdette, Milwaukee Braves pitcher, on hitters who chase bad pitches.*

167 If a horse can't eat it, I don't want to play on it. —*Dick Allen, St. Louis Cardinals infielder, on artificial surfaces.*

168   If a manager of mine ever said someone was indispensable, I'd fire him. — *Charley Finley, Oakland A's owner.*

169   If a man knows he's played bad ball and won't admit it, he shouldn't be out there. — *Leo Durocher, New York Giants manager.*

170   If any of my players don't take a drink now and then they'll be gone. You don't play this game on gingersnaps. — *Leo Durocher, Chicago Cubs manager.*

171   If anyone stays away, my response is this: Those people had no right to ever come to the park, because they aren't true baseball fans. — *George Brett, Kansas City Royals infielder, on fans who stay away from the park after the 1981 player strike.*

172   If a pitcher feels he has been intimidated by a hitter, he has a right to throw at him. — *Lynn McGlothen, St. Louis Cardinals pitcher.*

173   If a runner throws out his hand or his arm — even accidentally — and interferes with the pivot man's throw to first base on an attempted double play, both runners are out. But let him crash into some little shortstop or second baseman and deliberately break up the play, and he's just doing his job. It doesn't make sense. — *Frank Lane, Cleveland Indians general manager.*

174   If Bowie Kuhn were alive today, this strike never would have occurred. — *Peter Gammons, Boston Globe writer, on the 1981 player strike.*

175   I felt nothing. Nothing. — *Ted Williams, Boston Red Sox outfielder, asked how he felt during his last home run in his last game.*

176   Iffen you'd only a tole me you wuz gonna pitch a no-hitter, I'd a pitched me one, too. — *Dizzy Dean, St. Louis Cardinals pitcher, after brother Paul pitched a no-hitter to follow Dizzy's three-hitter.*

177   If I ain't startin', I ain't departin'. — *Garry Templeton, St. Louis Cardinals infielder, on the All-Star game.*

178   If I could straighten it out, I'd be pitching at Dodger Stadium tonight. — *Sandy Koufax, former Los Angeles Dodgers pitcher, when told to keep his arm straight while golfing.*

179   I find baseball fascinating. It strikes me as a native American ballet — a totally different dance form. Nearly every move in baseball — the wind-up, the pitch, the motion of the infielders — is different from other games. Next to a triple play, baseball's double play is the most exciting and graceful thing in sports. — *Alistair Cooke, reporter.*

180   If I had to name the number one asset you could have for any sport, I'd say speed. In baseball, all a guy with speed has to do is make contact. — *Ron Fairly, Los Angeles Dodgers infielder.*

181   If I'm breaking them, they're dying in style. — *John Mayberry, Kansas City Royals infielder, on his unusual number of broken bats.*

182   If I played there, they'd name a candy bar after me. — *Reggie Jackson, Oakland A's outfielder, on playing in New York City.*

183   I firmly believe if you want a boy to grow up and be a success in any line, you should teach him baseball, to have him understand it and play it. — *Leroy Collins, Florida governor.*

184   If I were playing third base and my mother were rounding third with the run that was going to beat us, I'd trip her. Oh, I'd pick her up and brush her off and say, "Sorry, Mom," but nobody beats me. — *Leo Durocher, former baseball manager.*

185   If life in general was a baseball game in the National or American League, this country wouldn't have these problems today. — *Roy Campanella, former Los Angeles Dodgers catcher, on integration.*

186   I found out a long time ago that there is no charity in baseball, and that every club owner must make his own fight for existence. — *Jacob Ruppert, New York Yankees owner, on a league profit-sharing plan during the Depression.*

187   If people don't come out to the ball park, who's going to stop them? — *Yogi Berra, New York Yankees coach.*

188   If pitching is 75 percent of baseball, it's 98 percent in the second game of a doubleheader. That's when depth really counts. — *Bob Sheffling, Milwaukee Braves.*

189   If someone's on the team, then he'll be good enough to play, because we've already proved that you can lose with anybody. — *Grady Hatton, Houston Astros manager.*

190   If they're losing $798,000, they might as well make it $799,000 and give me another $1,000. — *Alan Gallagher, San Francisco Giants infielder, on his contract with the financially-ailing team.*

191   If you aim to steal 30 or 40 bases a year, you do it by surprising the other side. But if your goal is 50 to a 100 bases, the element of surprise doesn't matter. You go even though they know you're going to go. Then each steal becomes a contest, matching your skills against theirs. — *Lou Brock, St. Louis Cardinals outfielder.*

192   If you can say the morale of your club is good after losing 10 out of 12 games, then your intelligence is a little low. — *Paul Richards, Baltimore Orioles manager.*

193   If you can't borrow it, steal it. — *Hugh E. Keough.*

194   If you can't do anything else, make a lot of noise. — *Ted Turner, Atlanta Braves owner.*

195   If you get to one base and you can see the ball on the ground in the outfield, run like hell to the next base. — *Zoilo Versalles, Minnesota Twins infielder, on running the bases.*

196   If you get 200 hits a season, you're going to hit .333 and you'll still have 400 outs. I don't see why you have to run down to first base every time to make an out. — *Bobby Bonds, New York Yankees outfielder, on striking out.*

197   If you're playing baseball and thinking about managing, you're crazy. You'd be better off thinking about being an owner. — *Casey Stengel, New York Yankees manager.*

198   If your stomach disputes you, lie down and pacify it with cool thoughts. — *Leroy (Satchel) Paige, Hall of Fame pitcher, on how to stay young.*

199   If you think it's an advantage, it is. If the other teams think it is, it's a bigger advantage. Actually, it means nothing. — *Jerry Reuss, Los Angeles Dodgers pitcher, on the value of experience in a pennant race.*

200   I had a better year. — *George Herman (Babe) Ruth, New York Yankees outfielder, on earning $80,000 a year compared to President Hoover's $75,000.*

201   I had one foot in the grave and the other on a banana peel. — *Wes Westrum, New York Mets manager, on his reason for resigning.*

202   I haven't missed a game in two and a half years. I go to the park sick as a dog and, when I see my uniform hanging there, I get well right now. Then I see some of you guys (the press), and I get sick again. — *Pete Rose, Cincinnati Reds infielder.*

203   I hit 'em when I want to; you hit 'em when you can. — *Alex Johnson, future Cincinnati Reds outfielder, to a minor league teammate.*

204   I hit 'em where they ain't. — *Willie Keeler, Brooklyn Dodgers outfielder.*

205   I kept hearing one guy talk about a "hard *slider*". Will somebody please tell me what a hard slider is? — *Frankie Frisch, former St. Louis Cardinals manager, on modern baseball announcers.*

206 I know a lot of players complain about night games, long flights and that stuff. I grant you that it's not easy, but it's not too hard either. There is no flight that takes longer than five hours. I wonder what some of those guys would say if they traveled by train like the old days. I can still feel those cinders and smell the smoke that came pouring in the open windows of those old Pullman cars. — *Jocko Conlon, retired umpire.*

207 I'll kill anybody that gets in my way. — *Ty Cobb, Detroit Tigers infielder.*

208 I'll never be considered one of the all-time greats, maybe not even one of the all-time goods. But I'm one of the all-time survivors. — *Jim Kaat, St. Louis Cardinals pitcher.*

209 I'll take any way to get into the Hall of Fame. If they want a batboy, I'll go in as a batboy. — *Phil Rizutto, former New York Yankees infielder.*

210 I'm always amazed when a pitcher becomes angry at a hitter for hitting a home run off him. When I strike out, I don't get angry at the pitcher, I get angry at myself. I would think that if a pitcher threw up a home run ball, he should be angry at himself. — *Willie Stargell, Pittsburgh Pirates infielder.*

211 I managed good, but boy did they play bad. — *Rocky Bridges, minor league manager, after losing his first game.*

212 I may have gone 0-for-4, made an error and cost us the game. But if a man and his wife come up to me with their kids, I can't help remembering my mom and dad taking me to the railing at the old ball park and hollering to get a player to sign an autograph. I remember how it felt. And how my parents felt as adults. I wouldn't offend those people for anything. — *Dal Maxvill, St. Louis Cardinals shortstop, on signing autographs.*

213 I'm 49 and I want to live to be 50. — *Eddie Sawyer, Philadelphia Phillies manager, retiring after the Phillies lost on opening day.*

214 I'm going to play with harder nonchalance this year. — *Jackie Brandt, Baltimore Orioles.*

215 I'm in the twilight of a mediocre career. — *Frank Sullivan, Boston Red Sox pitcher.*

216 I'm not going to quit a $60,000 to $70,000 job to go to work. — *Norm Cash, Detroit Tigers infielder.*

217 I'm not one of those old-timers who say everything was better in my day. I think ballplayers today are better than the players were when I played. But what ever happened to "sit down, shut up and listen?" — *Leo Durocher, former baseball manager.*

218 I'm not the manager because I'm always right, but I'm always right because I'm the manager. — *Gene Mauch, Montreal Expos manager.*

219 The important thing is that Denny McLain and Bob Gibson be household words, not Bowie Kuhn. The players are the game. The focus should be on them. — *Bowie Kuhn, commissioner of baseball.*

220 I'm still a Yankee fan and God knows that's a hard thing to be these days. — *Bishop Edwin Broderick, in 1969.*

221 I'm sure, I'm positive, I know there were people who changed their lives because of the Miracle Mets. People felt better. It was a good thing. — *Ed Charles, former New York Mets infielder, on the 1969 Miracle Mets.*

222 I'm throwing twice as hard, but the ball is getting there half as fast. — *Lefty Gomez, New York Yankees pitcher, on feeling the signs of age.*

223 In baseball, there is something electrifying about the big leagues. I had read so much about Musial, Williams and Robinson ... I had put those guys on a pedestal. They were something special ... I really thought that they put their pants on different, rather than one leg at a time. — *Henry Aaron, Atlanta Braves outfielder.*

224 I never called one wrong. — *Bill Klem, umpire.*

225 I never heard a crowd boo or hiss a homer, and I have heard plenty of boos after a strikeout. — *George Herman (Babe) Ruth, New York Yankees outfielder.*

226 I never knew how someone dying could say he was the luckiest man in the world. But now I understand. — *Mickey Mantle, New York Yankees outfielder, on his retirement day in Yankee Stadium.*

227 I never look back. I love baseball and you have to be patient and take the good with the bad. After all, it's only a game. — *Tom Yawkey, Boston Red Sox owner.*

228 In 10 years, Greg Goossen has a great chance of being 29 years old. — *Casey Stengel, New York Mets manager, on a 19-year-old player.*

229 In the back of every player's mind is the hope not to be the goat. — *Doug DeCinces, Baltimore Orioles infielder, on playing in the World Series.*

230 In this game of baseball, you live by the sword and die by it. You hit and get hit. Remember that. — *Alvin Dark, Cleveland Indians manager, on why the knock-down pitch will never leave.*

231 I once loved this game. But after being traded four times, I realize that it's nothing but a business. I treat my horses better than the owners treat us. It's a shame they've destroyed my love for the game. — *Dick Allen, Chicago White Sox infielder.*

232 I really love baseball. The guys and the game. And I love the challenge of describing things. The only thing I hate — and I know you have to be realistic and pay the bills in this life — is the loneliness of the road. — *Vin Scully, announcer.*

233 I regret I can't sit in the stands and watch me. — *Bo Belinsky, Philadelphia Phillies pitcher.*

234 I regret to this day that I never went to college. I feel I should have been a doctor. — *Ty Cobb, Detroit Tigers infielder.*

235 I remember the last season I played, I went home after a ball game one day, lay down on my bed, and the tears came to my eyes. How can you explain that? It's like crying for your mother after she's gone. You cry because you love her. I cried, I guess, because I loved baseball and I knew I had to leave it. — *Willie Mays, former New York Mets outfielder.*

236 Is Brooklyn still in the league? — *Bill Terry, New York Giants infielder.*

237 I signed Oscar Gamble on the advice of my attorney. I no longer have Oscar Gamble and I no longer have my attorney. — *Ray Kroc, San Diego Padres owner, on trading Oscar Gamble.*

238 I suspect that if a professional baseball player discovered one day that he could make more money by going back home and laying bricks for a living, he'd go home and lay bricks. — *Avery Brundage, Olympic president.*

239 I talk 'em out of hits. — *Lefty Gomez, New York Yankees pitcher.*

240 It doesn't take talent to be on time. — *Pete Reiser, California Angels coach.*

241 I think it's all right; it keeps the parents off the streets. — *Rocky Bridges, minor league manager, on little league baseball.*

242 I think most ballplayers read the sports pages, but I'm sorry to say that in most cases that's all they read. — *Ted Simmons, St. Louis Cardinals catcher.*

243 I thinks, me lads, this is me last slide. — *John (King) Kelly, record base stealer, on his death bed in 1894.*

244 I thought to myself, "It went away — it'll come back." But it never did. — *Sammy Ellis, minor league pitching coach, on his decline as a pitcher.*

245 It isn't the high price of stars that is expensive, it's the high price of mediocrity. — *Bill Veeck, Chicago White Sox owner.*

246 It is played by people. real people, not freaks. Basketball is played by giants. Football is played by corn-fed hulks. The normal-sized man plays baseball and the fellow in the stands can relate to that. — *Bill Veeck, Chicago White Sox owner, on baseball's being the national game.*

247 It looks like it's going to be a great season. — *Abner Doubleday, rumored founder of baseball.*

248 It's a league matter. — *Ford Frick, commissioner of baseball, when questioned on a problem.*

249 It's a long season and now that it's over, everybody can go home and have a good winter. — *James Brosnan, Cincinnati Reds pitcher.*

250 It's a lousy job. No matter who you pick, you're gonna be condemned. — *Billy Martin, All-Star game manager, on filling the squad.*

251 It's a mere moment in a man's life between an All-Star game and an old-timers game. — *Vin Scully, announcer.*

252 It's as inevitable as tomorrow, but perhaps not as imminent. — *Branch Rickey, baseball owner, on winning a championship.*

253 It's easy to stay in the majors for 7 and a half years when you hit .300. But when you hit .216, like me, it's really an accomplishment. — *Joe Lahoud, California Angels outfielder.*

254 It's great to be young and a Giant. — *Larry Doyle, New York Giants infielder.*

255 It's hard to win a pennant, but it's harder losing one. — *Chuck Tanner, Pittsburgh Pirates manager.*

256 It's just as important to know when not to go as it is to know when to go. — *Maury Wills, Los Angeles Dodgers infielder, on base stealing.*

257 It's like church. Many attend but few understand. — *Wes Westrum, San Francisco Giants coach, on baseball.*

258   It's making a man out of me. — *Ron Santo, Chicago Cubs infielder, on the team's slump.*

259   It's never over till it's over. — *Yogi Berra, New York Mets manager.*

260   It's no fun throwing fast balls to guys who can't hit them. The real challenge is getting them out on stuff they can hit. — *Sam McDowell, Cleveland Indians pitcher.*

261   It's not big if you look at it from the standpoint of the national debt. — *Bill Rigney, Minnesota Twins manager, on his team's high earned-run average.*

262   It's the only occupation I know where on the first day you must be perfect and them improve over the years. — *Grady Hatton, Houston Astros manager, on umpires.*

263   It's what you learn after you know it all that counts. — *Earl Weaver, Baltimore Orioles manager.*

264   It was a good play, but I gotta see him do it again. — *Charlie Dressen, Brooklyn Dodgers manager, after Willie Mays made a running catch, turned 360 degrees and threw out a runner at the plate.*

265   It will be a great honor if I'm voted in, but it's something a player should never expect will happen. — *Warren Spahn, former Milwaukee Braves pitcher, before joining the Hall of Fame.*

266   It will revolutionize baseball; it will open a new area of alibis for the players. — *Gabe Paul, baseball executive, on the Astrodome.*

267   I've always said I could manage Adolph Hitler, Benito Mussolini and Hirohito. That doesn't mean I'd like them, but I'd manage them. — *Billy Martin, New York Yankees manager.*

268   I've been with the club a year now and still haven't learned all the handshakes. — *Bob Miller, Pittsburgh Pirates pitcher.*

269   I've cheated, or someone on my team has cheated, in almost every game I've been in. — *Rogers Hornsby, St. Louis Cardinals infielder.*

270   I've heard of guys going 0-for-15, or 0-for-25, but I was 0-for-July. — *Bob Aspromonte, Houston Astros infielder.*

271   I've never met a perfect man and I know I'm going to miss one now and then. You just pray it doesn't happen in a big moment. The umpire who makes a bad call to blow a no-hitter is going to cry himself to sleep for the next 30 nights. — *Ron Luciano, umpire.*

272 I've seen the elephant, heard the owl and flown the screaming eagle. — *Bob Lemon, former New York Yankees pitcher, on being inducted into the Hall of Fame.*

273 I want a team that can get somebody out. — *Paul Richards, Baltimore Orioles manager.*

274 I want to be remembered as a ballplayer who gave all he had to give. — *Roberto Clementi, Pittsburgh Pirates outfielder.*

275 I want to pitch my way right into arbitration. — *Joe Decker, Minnesota Twins pitcher, on his goal for the season.*

276 I want to thank the good Lord, for making me a Yankee. — *Joe DiMaggio, New York Yankees outfielder, on Joe DiMaggio Day, 1949.*

277 I wasn't scared facing him because my father always told me I'd be another Koufax. — *Tug McGraw, New York Mets pitcher, after beating Sandy Koufax in his rookie season.*

278 I wish they'd shut the gates, and let us play ball with no press and no fans. — *Dick Allen, Philadelphia Phillies infielder.*

279 "I would like to take the great DiMaggio fishing," the old man said. "They say his father was a fisherman. Maybe he was as poor as we are and would understand." — *Ernest Hemingway, writer, in 'The Old Man and the Sea'.*

280 Kansas City fans don't know how to be mean. They know how to be mean in Philadelphia. — *Larry Bowa, Philadephia Phillies infielder, during the World Series against Kansas City.*

281 Keep the customers awake and you'll keep 'em coming. — *Larry McPhail, baseball executive, on baseball attendance.*

282 Keep the juices flowing by jangling around gently as you move. — *Leroy (Satchel) Paige, Hall of Fame pitcher, on the way to stay young.*

283 The key to a player's longevity in this game is his legs. He can hide such shortcomings as bad eyesight or slow reactions and cover them up for a couple years, but he can't hide bad legs. — *Rich Reichardt, Chicago White Sox infielder.*

284 The Kid doesn't chew tobacco, smoke, drink, curse or chase broads. I don't see how he can possibly make it. — *Richie Ashburn, Philadelphia Phillies announcer, on a rookie.*

285 Knowing all about baseball is just about as profitable as being a good whittler. — *Kin Hubbard.*

286 Last year they had four catchers out hurt and now they're going to bomb one. — *Mike Ryan, Philadelphia Phillies catcher, on catching the first ball of the season from a helicopter.*

287 Let him hit ya; I'll get you a new neck. — *Casey Stengel, New York Mets manager, to his hitter with the bases loaded.*

288 Let's have no secrets on this ball club. — *Bill Murray.*

289 Let's play two. — *Ernie Banks, Chicago Cubs infielder.*

290 Like all players, I enjoy recognition. And, I'm realistic. I know the minute I quit playing, no one will care. I'm going to live it up while I can. A year after I have quit, I'll be forgotten. — *Al Hrabosky, St. Louis Cardinals pitcher.*

291 The Lord taught me to love everybody. But the last ones the Lord taught me to love were the sports writers. — *Alvin Dark, Oakland A's manager.*

292 Losing streaks are funny. If you lose at the beginning, you got off to a bad start. If you lose in the middle of the season, you're in a slump. If you lose at the end, you're choking. — *Gene Mauch, Montreal Expos manager.*

293 Luck is the residue of design. — *Branch Rickey, baseball owner.*

294 The main quality a great third base coach must have is a fast runner. — *Rocky Bridges, California Angels coach.*

295 Major league baseball has done as much as any one thing in this country to keep up the spirit of the people. — *Franklin D. Roosevelt, President of the United States.*

296 Making the majors is not as hard as staying there, staying interested day after day. It's like being married. The hardest part is to stay married. — *Henry Aaron, Atlanta Braves outfielder.*

297 A manager really gets paid for how much he suffers. — *Gabe Paul, Cleveland Indians president.*

298 Managers are hired to be fired. — *Lefty Phillips, California Angels manager.*

299 Managing is not running, hitting, stealing. Managing is getting your players to put out 100 percent year after year. — *Sparky Anderson, Cincinnati Reds manager.*

300 Man may penetrate the outer reaches of the universe, he may solve the very secret of eternity itself, but for me, the ultimate human experience is to witness the flawless execution of the hit-and-run. — *Branch Rickey, baseball owner.*

301 The man who has the infinite capacity to take a bad situation and make it immediately worse. — *Branch Rickey, baseball owner, on Leo Durocher.*

302 The man with the ball is responsible for what happens to the ball. — *Branch Rickey, baseball owner, on whether the pitcher or catcher is responsible for pitching sequences.*

303 Maybe I'm not a great man, but I damn well want to break the record. — *Roger Maris, New York Yankees outfielder, on breaking Babe Ruth's 60 home run record.*

304 Me and my owners think exactly alike. Whatever they're thinking, that's what I'm thinking. — *Jim Fregosi, California Angels manager.*

305 The mental approach to pinch-hitting — to walk up there cold — is so different from playing regularly that it takes a special talent. Some of the games greatest haven't been able to handle it. Yet, men with .220 batting averages have been murder when sent up off the bench. I'll tell you this much: It's one of the toughest pressure jobs in baseball, because most of the time it means the ball game. — *Ralph Houk, New York Yankees manager.*

306 Morality at this point isn't a factor. — *Danny Ozark, Philadelphia Phillies manager, when asked about team morale during a slump.*

307 The most exciting hit in baseball is the triple.... You usually have two or three men handling the ball; and, if everything fits together, the runner is flagged down on a close play. On doubles and triples, several men must contribute. On a home run, one man does it all. — *Harry Walker, Houston Astros manager.*

308 Most one-run games are lost, not won. — *Gene Mauch, Philadelphia Phillies manager.*

309 The National League does not need New York. — *Warren Giles, National League president.*

310 The new ballparks are great and they hold a lot more people and the facilities are better. But the old parks had to have a charm we can't match today. — *Ted Simmons, St. Louis Cardinals catcher.*

311 Next thing you know, they'll be voting in Charlie McCarthy. He's a dummy, too, you know. All he ever did, for goodness sake, was saw logs. Why, he slept longer in office than ... Rip Van Winkle. — *Happy Chandler, former commissioner of baseball, on former commissioner Ford Frick's election into the Hall of Fame.*

312 Next to religion, baseball has furnished a greater impact on American life than any other institution. — *Herbert Hoover, President of the United States.*

313 Nice guys finish last. — *Leo Durocher, Brooklyn Dodgers manager.*

314 Nobody ever had too many of them. — *Casey Stengel, New York Yankees manager, on pitchers.*

315 Nobody goes there anymore, it's too crowded. — *Yogi Berra, New York coach, on a busy restaurant.*

316 Nobody knows how fast I am, the ball doesn't hit the mitt that often. — *Benny Daniels, Washington Senators pitcher, after being told he had a good fastball.*

317 Nobody should hit .200. Anybody should hit .250. — *Charley Lau, Kansas City Royals batting instructor.*

318 No manager ever thinks he got a break. I call them like I see them, and I don't care what team it is. If I'm right only half the time, I'm batting .500 — and I never saw a ball player bat .500. — *Jim Odom, umpire.*

319 No more than usual. — *Dick Stuart, Los Angeles Dodgers pitcher, asked if he was dizzy after being hit by a pitch.*

320 No sports event in our history has consistently captured the hearts of the public as much as the World Series. Traditionally, it has been the ultimate in sports competition. — *Bowie Kuhn, commissioner of baseball.*

321 No matter how long you have been playing, you still get butterflies before the big ones. — *Pee Wee Reese, Brooklyn Dodgers infielder.*

322 No matter how many errors you make, no matter how many times you strike out, keep hustling. That way you'll at least look like a ballplayer. — *Tony Kubek Sr. to New York Yankees rookie Tony Kubek Jr.*

323 No sweeping improvements, please. — *Harry Simmons, veteran outfielder.*

324 Not a bit; we lose at any altitude. — *Casey Stengel, New York Mets manager, asked if Mexico City's altitude bothered his team.*

325 Nuthin's new in baseball. — *Bill Stewart, umpire.*

326 Obviously the losers in the strike action taken tonight are the sports fans of America. — *Bowie Kuhn, commissioner of baseball, on the 1972 player strike.*

327 Of such pleasing incidents is the pastime made up. — *Charles Dryden.*

328 One reason I have always loved baseball so much is that it has been not merely the "great national game," but really a part of the whole weather of our lives, of the thing that is our own, of the whole fabric, the million memories of America. — *Tom Wolfe, writer.*

329 One thing all managers hear that doesn't make any sense at all is for the pitcher to say, "I ought to have a right to stay in and win or lose my own game. He doesn't have that right. It isn't just his game. There are 24 other players who have a stake in it, plus the managers and coaches and everybody else in the organization. All have worked to field the team and are affected by what happens. — *Harry Walker, Houston Astros manager.*

330 One year I hit .291 and had to take a salary cut. If you hit .291 today, you'd own the franchise. — *Enos Slaughter, former Pittsburgh Pirate.*

331 The one change is that baseball has turned Paige from a second-class citizen into a second-class immortal. — *Leroy (Satchel) Paige, pitcher, on being inducted into the Hall of Fame's Negro section.*

332 The only real happiness a ballplayer has is when he is playing a ball game and accomplishes something he didn't think he could do. — *Ring Lardner, writer.*

333 The only thing I believe is this: A player does not have to like a manager and he does not have to respect a manager. All he has to do is obey the rules. — *Sparky Anderson, Cincinnati Reds manager.*

334 The only thing wrong with the Mets is that we don't play them enough. — *George Kirksey, Houston Astros vice president in 1965.*

335 The one thing wrong with our pitchers is they all have to pitch the same night. — *Don Osborn, Pittsburgh Pirates coach.*

336 The only way to make progress is to make more progress. — *Branch Rickey, baseball owner.*

337 The only way you can get along with newspapermen is to say something one minute and something different the next. — *Hank Greenberg, Detroit Tigers infielder.*

338   On the lowest farms we have just one manager. Where we have the most need for teachers, we have the fewest, and where we need the fewest teachers, we have the most. This will have to change. — *Heywood Sullivan Boston Red Sox personnel director.*

339   On this day I consider myself the luckiest man on the face of the earth. — *Lou Gehrig, New York Yankees outfielder, on Lou Gehrig Day, July 4, 1939.*

340   Opening day to closing day, you belong to me. — *Eddie Stanky, Chicago White Sox manager, to his players.*

341   The other teams could make trouble for us if they win. — *Yogi Berra, New York Yankees manager.*

342   Our pitching staff is a conspiracy of ifs. — *Branch Rickey, St. Louis Cardinals manager.*

343   Owning the Yankees is like owning the Mona Lisa. That's something you never sell. — *George Steinbrenner, New York Yankees owner, on whether he would sell the team.*

344   Papa Bell was so fast, he could turn out the light and jump in bed before the room got dark. — *Leroy (Satchell) Paige, Hall of Fame pitcher, on James (Cool Papa) Bell.*

345   The papers aren't going to win a game for me. And I don't need anyone to tell me I lost. — *Harry Walker, Houston Astros manager, on why he refuses to read newspaper articles on his team.*

346   People identify with swashbuckling individuals, not polite little men who field their position well. Sir Galahad had a big following — but I'll bet Lancelot had more. — *Bill Veeck, Chicago White Sox owner.*

347   People who write about spring training not being necessary have never tried to throw a baseball. — *Sandy Koufax, Los Angeles Dodgers pitcher.*

348   Percentage baseball must be good. If it weren't, it wouldn't work so often. — *Michael (Pinky) Higgins, Boston Red Sox manager.*

349   Philly fans are so mean that one Easter Sunday, when the players staged an Easter egg hunt for the kids, the fans booed the kids who didn't find any eggs. — *Bob Uecker, former Philadelphia Phillies catcher.*

350 A pitcher has to look at the hitter as his mortal enemy. — *Early Wynn, Chicago White Sox pitcher.*

351 Pitchers did me a favor when they knocked me down. It made me more determined. I wouldn't let that pitcher get me out. They say you can't hit if you're on your back. But I didn't hit on my back. I got up. — *Frank Robinson, former Baltimore Orioles outfielder.*

352 Pitching is really just an internal struggle between the pitcher and his stuff. If my curve ball is breaking and I'm throwing it where I want, then the batter is irrelevent. — *Steve Stone, Baltimore Orioles pitcher.*

353 Players are the most helpless people in the world. If you told them to get to San Francisco by themselves, they might end up in Mexico City. — *Tom Yawkey, Boston Red Sox owner.*

354 Players believe the mystique about big-league baseball probably more than kids or fans do. It's those two words that are not applied to any other sport — big league. — *Wes Parker, Los Angeles Dodgers infielder.*

355 Players have lost all loyalty to a club, to their teammates and perhaps even to themselves. — *Buzzie Bavasi, baseball executive.*

356 Players who create controversy are winning players who can perform under pressure. — *Gabe Paul, New York Yankees general manager.*

357 Playing baseball for a living is like having a license to steal. — *Pete Rose, Cincinnati Reds infielder.*

358 The premium on sound judgment is enormous in a climate of soaring costs. — *Bowie Kuhn, commissioner of baseball.*

359 Pressure? Well, it ain't hitting in 44 straight games, because I done that and it was fun. The playoffs are pressure. — *Pete Rose, Philadelphia Phillies infielder.*

360 Prospects are a dime a dozen. — *Charley Finley, Oakland A's owner.*

361 The reason the Yankees never lay an egg is because they don't operate on chicken feed. — *Dan Parker, writer.*

362 Right now, 10 percent of the baseball players are making all the money. The rest are jealous. — *Joe Burke, Kansas City Royals general manager.*

363 Rooting for the Yankees is like rooting for U.S. Steel. — *Red Smith, announcer.*

364 The rules are changed now. There's not any way to build a team today. It's just how much money you want to spend. You could be the world champions, and somebody else makes a key acquisition or two and you're through. — *Whitey Herzog, Kansas City Royals manager.*

365 Say it ain't so, Joe. — *Anonymous boy, begging Joe Jackson to say he had not thrown the 1919 World Series.*

366 The secret of managing a club is to keep the five guys who hate you away from the five who are undecided. — *Casey Stengel, New York Mets manager.*

367 A sense of humor and a good bullpen. — *Whitey Herzog, Kansas City Royals manager, on the ingredients of a successful manager.*

368 Show me a good loser in professional sports and I'll show you an idiot. Show me a sportsman and I'll show you a player I'm looking to trade. — *Leo Durocher, baseball manager.*

369 Shouting on a ball field never helped anyone except when it was one player calling to another to take the catch. — *Gil Hodges, New York Mets manager.*

370 The sign of a good hitter is when you look for it, get it, and send it. — *Brooks Robinson, former Baltimore Orioles infielder.*

371 Sittin' in the cat bird seat. — *Red Barber, announcer, when the Dodgers were in first place.*

372 Sixty, count 'em, sixty. Let's see some other son-of-a-bitch match that. — *George Herman (Babe) Ruth, New York Yankees outfielder, after hitting his 60th home run.*

373 Some teams never win. They've got four or five guys who never care about anything. They don't want the grind of the full six months. As soon as things start to go bad, they crack and just go for themselves. Talent is one thing. Being able to go from spring to October is another. — *Sparky Anderson, Cincinnati Reds manager.*

374 Sometimes I have this fantasy: The manager's been popping off all day and his team's just blown a big lead. I call time and walk over to the dugout and say very politely, "Excuse me, sir. Your second baseman just booted one with the bases loaded." — *Nestor Chylak, umpire.*

375 Sometimes I really think it's better to be a mediocre player in the big leagues instead of a star. They seem to last longer. — *Frank Robinson, former Baltimore Orioles outfielder.*

376 Son, we'd like to keep you around this season, but we're going to try to win a pennant. — *Casey Stengel, New York Yankees manager, to a rookie.*

377 Spread out, guys, so they can't get all of us with one shot. — *Frank Sullivan, Philadelphia Phillies pitcher, seeing a crowd as the team deplaned during a losing streak.*

378 Stay with them for a few more innings until I think of something. — *Charley Dressen, Los Angeles Dodgers manager, during a close game.*

379 Sure I do, and if someone paid you $6,000 a game, you'd have fun as well. — *Pete Rose, Philadelphia Phillies infielder, asked if he had fun playing baseball.*

380 Sure it's nice to win; but there is only one thing that's important to me and that's the money that we're going to get, win or lose. It's a business with me, and I refuse to lie to all the Little Leaguers and try to con them. I don't love baseball, I like it. And to me baseball means money, and that's all I care about. — *Vida Blue, Oakland A's pitcher, after winning the Western Division.*

381 Sweat is your only salvation. — *Fred Hutchinson, St. Louis Cardinals manager.*

382 Take nothing for granted in baseball. — *Harry Pulliam, National League president.*

383 The team that gets off to a good start wins pennants. — *John McGraw, New York Giants manager.*

384 The team that wins two-thirds of its one-run games usually wins the pennant. — *Pete Rose, Cincinnati Reds infielder.*

385 That is what makes baseball the great game that it is. — *Bill Mazeroski, Pittsburgh Pirate infielder, asked what he thought of a rookie swearing at him during the game.*

386 That's very disturbing. — *Danny Ozark, Philadelphia Phillies manager, told his team was seven games behind with six to play.*

387 That's what it means to be an umpire. You have to be honest even when it hurts. — *Doug Harvey, umpire, after one of the crew admitted a mistake.*

388 There are always problem players and there is always someone who feels he can handle them. — *Dick Walsh, California Angels general manager.*

389 There are a lot of things I can do that I haven't done yet. Until I do them, I'm short-changing myself, the fans and our owner. — *Reggie Jackson, Oakland A's outfielder.*

390 There are cases when a crowd should boo a player; like when it's obvious he isn't trying. But the kind of booing that gets me is when you're going bad and the fans get on you. It doesn't help. It never helps to get booed when you're trying. — *Bob Bailey, Montreal Expos infielder.*

391 There are certain players in this league who should never — I mean never — get a key hit against you. — *Gene Mauch, Philadelphia Phillies manager.*

392 There are things about some professional athletes that I cannot stand — the pretense, the egos, the pomposity, the greed. — *Ted Simmons, St. Louis Cardinals catcher.*

393 There are things you can do when you have talent that are colorful. If you do them without talent, they're bush. — *Gabe Paul, Cleveland Indians general manager.*

394 There are two theories on hitting the knuckleball. Unfortunately, neither of them work. — *Charlie Lau, Chicago White Sox coach.*

395 There has always been a saying in baseball that you can't make a hitter. But I think you can improve a hitter. More than you can improve a fielder. More mistakes are made hitting than in any other part of the game. — *Ted Williams, Boston Red Sox outfielder.*

396 There is a distinct lack of concern on the part of management. It's paranoia on their part. They want to keep it quiet and out of the newspapers. They want you to believe that nothing like this could happen in their organization. — *Don Newcombe, former Brooklyn Dodgers pitcher, on management's attempt to stop alcohol abuse.*

397 There is no doubt that someone who tries to throw a curve or pitch at an early age before he's developed, before his hand is big enough to grip the ball correctly, will damage his arm. — *Robin Roberts, former Philadelphia Phillies pitcher.*

398 There is one word in America that says it all, and that one word is, "You never know." — *Joaquin Andujar, Houston Astros pitcher.*

399 There is only one legitimate trick to pinch-hitting, and that's knowing the pitcher's best pitch when the count is 3-and-2. All the rest is a crapshoot. —*Earl Weaver, Baltimore Orioles manager.*

400 There should be a new way to record standings in this league: one column for wins, one for losses and one for gifts. —*Gene Mauch, Philadelphia Phillies manager.*

401 There's no meaning to this honor if you're not alive. —*Earl Averill, at hit induction into the Hall of Fame.*

402 There's no such thing as pressure. It's all in your mind. But if there were such a thing as pressure, it would be the worst in the playoffs. The playoffs are just a mother. —*Earl Weaver, Baltimore Orioles manager.*

403 There's nothing wrong with this club that a few wins won't cure. —*Anonymous.*

404 There's the Hall of Fame and there's the Hall of Achievement and there's also the Hall of Enjoyment. I just hope to be enshrined in the Hall of Enjoyment for a bit longer. —*Jim Kaat, St. Louis Cardinals pitcher, on how long he would like to continue playing.*

405 There was a day when the special covenants in a player contract took up about four inches. Now they go for pages. —*Phil Seghi, Cleveland Indians general manager.*

406 There was only one man in the world who was perfect, and they crucified him. —*Jack Powell, Pacific League umpire supervisor.*

407 These are the saddest possible words, Tinkers-to-Evers-to-Chance. —*Franklin Adams, writer, on the Chicago Cubs double play trio.*

408 They ain't nothin' till I call them. —*Bill Klem, umpire, on pitches.*

409 They can't come back. The doors are closed to them for good. The most scandalous chapter in the game's history is closed. —*James Landis, commissioner of baseball, on the Chicago Black Sox.*

410 They look like that gang that hangs around down by the gashouse. —*Joe Val, sports editor, on the 1935 St. Louis Cardinals.*

411 They never cried for us and you can bet your tail we're not crying for them. —*Sam Mele, Minnesota Twins manager, on the decline of the 1965 New York Yankees.*

412 They ought to change our name to the Cleveland Light Company. We don't have anything but utilitymen. —*Lou Camilli, Cleveland Indians infielder.*

413 They ought to make a rule that if a guy gets hit and is able to get up, they should tie the pitcher's hands behind his back and let the hitter smack him in the face. — *Dan Thomas, Milwaukee Brewers infielder.*

414 They're not the greatest ball club I've ever seen, but they think they are. — *Joe Gordon, Cleveland Indians manager, on his team's fast start.*

415 They say Lyndon Johnson can remember your name five years later. I might not know yours next week, but I can remember everything I ever saw a player do. — *Grady Hatton, Houston Astros manager.*

416 They say some of my stars drink whiskey, but I have found that the ones who drink milkshakes don't win many ball games. — *Casey Stengel, New York Yankees manager.*

417 They say you have to be good to be lucky, but I think you have to be lucky to be good. — *Rico Carty, Atlanta Braves outfielder.*

418 They still can't steal first base. — *Phil Rizzuto, New York Yankees infielder.*

419 They've got a lot of names for pitches now, but there are only so many ways you can throw a baseball. — *Pete Reiser, Chicago Cubs coach.*

420 The thing about starting fast is it gives you something to bob and weave with for the rest of the season. — *Ralph Garr, Atlanta Braves outfielder.*

421 This is reaching the top. That's what we all strive for no matter what profession we're in. I feel that my life is fulfilled now. — *Lou Boudreau, former Cleveland Indians infielder, on his induction to the Hall of Fame.*

422 This strike was never for the Hank Aarons, Carl Yastrzemskis or Willie Mayses. It was for the four-year players who pass up college, spend three to five years to make the majors and have a career ruined by a dead arm or leg. — *Howard Cosell, announcer, on the 1972 player strike.*

423 Throwing a fastball by Henry Aaron is like trying to sneak the sun past a rooster. — *Curt Simmons, Philadelphia Phillies pitcher.*

424 To compare baseball with other team games is to say the Hope Diamond is a nice chunk of carbon. The endless variety of physical and mental skills demanded by baseball is both uncomparable and incomparable. — *Bill Veeck, former owner.*

425 Today's athletes run faster and make a lot more plays in the field. But the name of the game is still pitching and it ain't going to change. Pitching was 80 percent of baseball when John McGraw managed and it's still 80 percent of baseball. — *Paul Richards, Chicago White Sox manager.*

426   A torn rotator cuff is a cancer for a pitcher. And if a pitcher gets a badly torn one, he has to face the facts: It's all over, baby. — *Don Drysdale, former Los Angeles Dodgers pitcher.*

427   Trade a player a year too early rather than a year too late. — *Branch Rickey, baseball owner.*

428   The trouble with some pitchers these days is that they don't know the difference between an ache and a pain. One needs work and the other needs rest. — *Mayo Smith, Detroit Tigers manager.*

429   A .220 hitter in the minors will be a .220 hitter all his life. — *Marty Marion, St. Louis Cardinals coach.*

430   The umpires have kept this game honest for 100 years. We're the only segment of the game that has never been touched by scandal. We've got to be too dumb to cheat. We must have integrity, because we sure don't have a normal family life. We certainly aren't properly paid. We have no health care, no job security, no tenure. Our pension plan is a joke. We take more abuse than any living group of humans, and can't give any back. If we're fired without notice, our only recourse is to appeal to the league president. And he's the guy that fires you. If you ask for one day off in the seven month season, they try to make you feel three inches tall. If you call in sick, you're hounded and ostracized by the brass. Umpires must be the healthiest people on earth, because none of us ever gets sick. — *Ron Luciano, umpire.*

431   Under generally accepted accounting procedures, I can turn a $4 million profit into a $2 million dollar loss, and I could get every national accounting firm to agree with me. — *Paul Beeston, Toronto Blue Jays vice president.*

432   Under pressure, you want to be at peace with yourself. You want your energy to flow, not feel knotted. You don't want to be too sharp. You don't want to be too flat. You just want to be natural. — *Willie Stargell, Pittsburgh Pirates infielder.*

433   Very few managers can remain when they're in ninth place unless they can tell a lot of jokes. And I can't tell a lot of jokes. — *Eddie Stanky, Chicago White Sox manager, on being fired.*

434   The way to catch a knuckleball is to wait until the ball stops rolling and then pick it up. — *Bob Uecker, announcer.*

435   We Americans are a peculiar people. We are for the underdog no matter how much of a dog he is. — *Happy Chandler, commissioner of baseball.*

436   We can't always guarantee the ball game is going to be good; but we can guarantee the fan will have fun. — *Bill Veeck, Chicago White Sox president.*

437 We hit the dry side of the ball. — *Gene Oliver, Milwaukee Braves infielder, on how to hit a spitball.*

438 We'll continue to play by baseball rules. — *Chub Feeney, National League president, on the refusal to adopt the designated hitter in 1973.*

439 Well, that's football. — *Ray Fosse, Cleveland Indians catcher, after being injured after colliding with Pete Rose in the 1970 All-Star game.*

440 We're not going to give them another God damn cent. — *Gussie Busch, St. Louis Cardinals owner, on player pension benefits during the 1972 player strike.*

441 What, and give him a chance to think on my time. — *Grover Cleveland Alexander, St. Louis Cardinals pitcher, on why he doesn't take more time on the mound.*

442 What I wonder is, where are the guys who just love to play baseball? — *Wes Parker, former Los Angeles Dodgers infielder.*

443 When a man asks you to come and see baseball played twice, it sets you to asking yourself why you went to see it played once. — *George Bernard Shaw, writer.*

444 When I first came up as a manager I was too damn demanding. I had to learn never to expect a man to do something he is not capable of doing. Now I try to analyze and find out their capabilities and then never ask to exceed them. — *Danny Murtaugh, Pittsburgh Pirates manager.*

445 When I first signed with the Yankees, the regulars wouldn't talk to you until you were with the team three or four years. Nowadays, the rookies get $100,000 to sign and they don't talk to the regulars. — *Lefty Gomez, New York Yankees pitcher.*

446 When I played, they didn't use fancy words like that. They just said I couldn't hit. — *Bob Uecker, announcer, on players who claim 'emotional distress' affects their game.*

447 When I was a small boy in Kansas, a friend of mine and I went fishing and as we sat there in the warmth of the summer afternoon on a river bank, we talked about what we wanted to do when we grew up. I told him that I wanted to be a real major league baseball player, a genuine professional like Honus Wagner. My friend said that he'd like to be president of the United States. Neither of us got our wish. — *Dwight Eisenhower, President of the United States.*

448 When I was managing Brooklyn I'd have to stop at this light each day on the way home. On the corner was a bar, and the guys would always yell, "Hey, Leo, who won?" If I said, "Us", they'd say great going. If I said, "Them", they'd call me a dumb sonofabitch. — *Leo Durocher, former Brooklyn Dodgers manager.*

449 When somebody on your team does that, you say, "What guts. What a gamer". When a guy on the other team does it, you say, "What a dummy. There's no percentage in that". When it's the other guy, you become a cynic. — *Ray Miller, Baltimore Orioles coach, after a player made a catch while running into the wall.*

450 When the one great scorer comes to mark against your name, it's not whether you won or lost but how many paid to see the game. — *Peter Bavasi, Toronto Blue Jays general manager.*

451 When we lose I can't sleep at night. When we win I can't sleep at night. But when you win you wake up feeling better. — *Joe Torre, New York Mets manager.*

452 When we played, World Series checks meant something. Now all they do is screw up your taxes. — *Don Drysdale, announcer.*

453 When you can do it out there between the white lines, you can live any way you want. — *Denny McLain, Detroit Tigers pitcher.*

454 When you first sign that contract as a kid, they tell you your whole future is ahead of you. But they forget to tell you that your future stops at 35. — *Hal Jeffcoat, St. Louis Cardinals pitcher.*

455 When you're doing it, when you're hitting home runs, you can get away with anything. But when you're not delivering, it won't work. They won't buy your act. — *Ken Harrelson, former Boston Red Sox outfielder.*

456 When you're 21, you're a prospect. When you're 30, you're a suspect. — *Jim McGlothlin, Chicago White Sox pitcher.*

457 When you're winning, beer tastes better. — *Jimmie Dykes, Detroit Tigers manager.*

458 Where you position yourself before the pitch, and the first two steps you take after the ball is hit are the only things that count now. — *Gene Mauch, Montreal Expos manager, on fielding on artificial surfaces.*

459 Whoever wants to know the heart and mind of America had better learn baseball. — *Jacques Barzun, educator.*

460   Why do I have to be an example for your kid? You be an example for your own kid. — *Bob Gibson, St. Louis Cardinals pitcher.*

461   Why should I throw at him for getting a few hits off me? When I strike him out three times a game, does he try to throw his bat at me? — *Steve Stone, Baltimore Orioles pitcher, on throwing at hitters.*

462   A win in April is just as important as a win in September. — *Dave Bristol, Cincinnati Reds manager.*

463   With all the glamour attached to hitting the ball out of the park, it takes a lot of discipline to go up there and just try to get a base hit. — *Garry Maddox, Philadelphia Phillies outfielder.*

464   The worst thing is the day you realize you want to win more than the players do. — *Gene Mauch, Minnesota Twins manager, speaking to a rookie manager.*

465   The Yankees don't pay me to win every day — just two out of three. — *Casey Stengel, New York Yankees manager.*

466   Yes, we can. — *Dave Cash, Philladelphia Phillies infielder.*

467   Yogi (Berra), you better tell your pitcher to start pitching me outside or I'm going to start pitching you inside. — *Early Wynn, Chicago White Sox pitcher, after taking a knock-down pitch.*

468   You always get a special kick on opening day, no matter how many you go through. You look forward to it like a birthday party when you're a kid. You think something wonderful is going to happen. — *Joe DiMaggio, New York Yankees outfielder.*

469   You can go to the ball park on a quiet Tuesday afternoon, with only a few thousand people in the place, and thoroughly enjoy a one-sided game. Baseball has an esthetic, intellectual appeal found in no other team sport. — *Bowie Kuhn, commissioner of baseball.*

470   You can have money piled up to the ceiling, but the size of your funeral is still going to depend on the weather. — *Chuck Tanner, Pittsburgh Pirates manager, on high salaries.*

471   You can only milk a cow so long, then you're left holding the pail. — *Henry Aaron, Milwaukee Brewers outfielder, announcing his retirement.*

472   You can shake a dozen glove men out of a tree, but the bat separates the men from the boys. — *Dale Long, Washington Senators infielder.*

473 You can't be thinking about too many things. Relief pitchers have to get into a zone of their own. I just hope I'm stupid enough. — *Dan Quisenberry, Kansas City Royals pitcher.*

474 You can't fire me, I quit. — *Joe Gordon, Cleveland Indians manager, on being fired.*

475 You can't get rich sitting on a bench — but I'm giving it a try. — *Phil Linz, New York Yankees infielder.*

476 You can't hit what you can't see. — *Walter Johnson, Washington Senators pitcher, on his fastball.*

477 You can't tell how much spirit a team has until it starts losing. — *Rocky Colavito, Detroit Tigers outfielder.*

478 You can't win them all. — *Connie Mack, Philadelphia A's manager, after his team lost 117 games.*

479 You don't save a pitcher for tomorrow. Tomorrow it may rain. — *Leo Durocher, manager.*

480 You gotta be careful with your body. Your body is like a bar of soap. The more you use it, the more it wears down. — *Dick Allen, Chicago White Sox infielder.*

481 You gotta keep the ball off the fat part of the bat. — *Leroy (Satchel) Paige, Hall of Fame pitcher, on his pitching philosophy.*

482 You have no idea the pressure a young pitcher is under. I've walked out to the mound in the middle of an inning and the pitcher couldn't tell me his telephone number. By walking out, you calm him down.... Yelling at a boy from the bench is confusing and ridiculous. — *Johnny Sain, pitching coach.*

483 You have to be a man, but you have to have a lot of little boy in you, too. — *Roy Campanella, Brooklyn Dodgers catcher, on what it takes to be a major leaguer.*

484 You have to draft a catcher, because if you don't have one, the pitch will roll all the way back to the screen. — *Casey Stengel, New York Mets manager, on why his first draft choice was an unknown catcher.*

485 You have two alternatives. You can play in Philadelphia or you can quit. — *Marvin Miller, Players Association director, when Steve Carlton asked for his options after being traded.*

486 You may go a long time without winning, but you never forget that scent. — *Steve Busby, Kansas City Royals pitcher.*

487 You mix two jiggers of scotch to one jigger of Metrecal. So far I've lost five pounds and my drivers license. — *Rocky Bridges, minor league manager, on his diet formula.*

488 You must try to generate happiness within yourself. If you aren't happy in one place, chances are you won't be happy any place. — *Ernie Banks, Chicago Cubs infielder.*

489 You never unpack your suitcases in this business. — *Preston Gomez, baseball manager, after being fired.*

490 The youngsters coming up now just go through the motions necessary to make the play. They should bounce around a little, show some life and zip. It adds a little action and gives the fans something to look at — rather than the monotonous routine, no matter how perfectly the play is made. — *Al Lopez, Chicago White Sox manager.*

491 You only miss a winner; or a loser that's got a lot of heart. — *Arthur Van Allen, hotel doorman, on the possible move of the San Francisco Giants.*

492 You pick up the paper sometimes and read where a player says, "I can't play for this manager". Makes me laugh. You don't play for the manager, you play for the team. This is who I play for. I play for 24 other players, the manager and the trainer — everybody on the team. — *Pete Rose, Cincinnati Reds infielder.*

493 You should do everything possible to win short of scratching the other guy's eyes out. — *Ken Aspromonte, Cleveland Indians manager.*

494 You're trying your damndest, you strike out and they boo you. I act like it doesn't bother me, like I don't hear anything the fans say, but the truth is I hear every word of it and it kills me. — *Mike Schmidt, Philadelphia Phillies infielder.*

495 You usually can tell who's not going to make it. But when a scout tells you a player "Can't miss", don't listen. — *Paul Richards, baseball scout.*

496 You've got to be careful. Most writers are good guys, but there's always one in a crowd, one who tries to quote you out of context, to make you look bad, and you've got to look around for him. Sometimes you can spot him, sometimes you can't. But you've always got to be careful. — *Al Kaline, Detroit Tigers outfielder.*

497 You want experience and the real pros for the All-Star game. If you

had one race to win, which would you pick — Man o' War or his offspring?
— *George Selkirk, Washington Senators general manager, on why career and not just season performance should select All-Stars.*

Basketball

498   The ability to prepare to win is as important as the will to win. — *Bobby Knight, Indiana basketball coach.*

499   Adolph (Rupp) has won 800 and some games. Five hundred of them have been against Southeastern Conference teams. That's like me going down to Texas with six kids from Canada and starting a hockey league. — *Johnny Dee, Notre Dame basketball coach.*

500   After about two months into the season, you see your relative position on a team and you accept it. You might not like it, but you accept it. — *Bill Hosket, New York Knickerbockers forward, on being a reserve.*

501   All I do is coach and put my players on the floor. If they win, fine. If they lose, it's their fault. — *Abe Lemons, Texas basketball coach.*

502   All I want out of life is to get a bunch of boys together and whip somebody else. — *Adolph Rupp, Kentucky basketball coach.*

503   Anytime you pass up a $100,000 or so, that's a hardship. — *Frank Oleynick, Seattle guard, on how he could declare himself a hardship case for the NBA draft.*

504   Ask a rookie the difference between the regular season and the playoffs, and he'll tell you it's that he didn't play in the playoffs. — *Bill Fitch, Boston Celtics coach.*

505   The appeal of basketball is that it is an easy game to play, but difficult to master. — *James Naismith, founder of basketball.*

506   At a tournament like this you find out who's closer to God. — *Fred Handler, St. Bonaventure assistant basketball coach, on the NCAA tournament.*

507   The athlete approaches the end of his playing days the way old people approach death. But the athlete differs from the old person in that he must continue living. Behind all the years of practice and all the hours of glory waits that inexorable terror of living without the game. — *Bill Bradley, former New York Knickerbockers forward.*

508 Athletics opens doors, but you're in trouble if you depend on those open doors alone. — *Willie Naulls, UCLA basketball player.*

509 Basketball is elbows. — *Lucias Mitchell, Kentucky State basketball coach.*

510 Basketball was fun in high school, but you find as you get into the big time college ball that it gets to be a business and less pleasure. — *Darryl Brown, Fordham basketball coach.*

511 Bavetta, if you had another eye, you'd be a cyclops. — *Anonymous fan to NBA referee Dick Bavetta.*

512 Cal passes and passes and then takes the same shot they had 15 minutes ago. — *Johnny Green, UCLA guard, on the California offense.*

513 Coaching is the greatest opportunity a man can have if he wants to be a teacher — a teacher who gets to see the progress of what he's teaching happening right before him. — *Marv Harshman, Washington basketball coach.*

514 A coach is a teacher, and like any good teacher, I'm trying to build men. — *John Wooden, UCLA basketball coach.*

515 Coaching is easy. Winning is the hard part. — *Elgin Baylor, New Orleans Jazz coach.*

516 Coaching is just a matter of getting rid of the bad apples. — *Dick Motta, Chicago Bulls coach.*

517 College is fun, but sometimes it's too much fun. I just got caught up in the fun. — *Johnny Crawford, Kansas forward, on being declared academically ineligible.*

518 Defeat is worse than death because you have to live with defeat. — *Bill Musselman, Minnesota basketball coach.*

519 Discipline is the most important thing in life. — *Bill Musselman, Minnesota basketball coach.*

520 Doesn't matter how you feel, the cows have to be milked. — *Bill Andreas, Ohio State basketball player, on why he played in a game injured.*

521 Don't get 'em to like you, get 'em to respect you. — *Mendy Rudolph, referee, on his philosophy.*

522 Don't play much defense, do you, Dick? — *Bill Sharman, All-Star guard, to Dick Garmaker after making an 80-foot basket in the 1957 All-Star game.*

523 The dreary march to the foul line does less for basketball than anything I can think of. — *George Mikan, American Basketball Association president.*

524 An 80-foot jumper. (Pause) Good. — *Chick Hearn, announcer, when Jerry West hit a court length shot in the playoffs.*

525 Elg is the kind of guy that when he's not around, you know he's not around. — *Jerry West, Los Angeles Lakers guard, on teammate Elgin Baylor.*

526 Eliminate the referees, raise the basket four feet, double the size of the basketball, limit the height of the players to 5-9, bring back the center jump, allow taxi drivers in free and allow the players to carry guns. — *Al McGuire, announcer, on ways to make basketball more exciting.*

527 Enforcers are vital. They are part of the game by whatever name you call them. Basketball is not a non-contact sport. You have to have someone who loves contact and is willing to keep order. — *Pete Newell, Los Angeles Lakers general manager, on the importance of a power player.*

528 Everybody on a championship team doesn't get publicity, but everybody can say he's a champion. — *Earvin (Magic) Johnson, Los Angeles Lakers guard.*

529 Every fan in the nation now is conscious of how basketball can and should be played. — *Bill Walton, Portland Trailblazers center, after winning the NBA championship.*

530 Every obnoxious fan has a wife home who dominates him. — *Al McGuire, Marquette basketball coach.*

531 Every team has a pair of top players, but its the third man down who wins and loses games. — *Del Harris, Houston Rockets basketball coach.*

532 Fans never fall asleep at our games because they're afraid they might get hit with a pass. — *George Raveling, Washington State basketball coach.*

533 The fans said we couldn't pass, couldn't run, couldn't dribble and didn't hustle ... They are just like fans all over — picky, picky, picky. — *Gary Hulst, Montana State basketball coach, on his 4-22 team.*

534 The floor we've got was built for 6-footers, not for athletes over six-four or five. Today, we've got over 100 seven-footers and we're long overdue in making adjustments. It is so crowded out there now that it's almost war. — *Press Maravich, LSU basketball coach, on enlarging the court.*

535 A former teammate of mine told me that we have, as a team, the collective intelligence of an orangutan. I cannot say that I disagree. *— Phil Jackson, New York Knickerbockers forward.*

536 Fortunately, in each championship game we were usually ahead enough right near the end so I could call a time-out in the last few minutes. During these time-outs, I reaffirmed to everyone that when the game was over we shouldn't act like fools. I told them it was a basketball game, and nothing more. *— John Wooden, former UCLA basketball coach.*

537 Genius is perseverance in disguise. *— Mike Newlin, New York Nets guard.*

538 Give the players all the money they deserve, but don't guarantee it. Don't tell them they don't have to work for it. When you eliminate motivation, you eliminate competition, you eliminate accomplishment. *— Bob Cousy, Cincinnati basketball coach.*

539 A good pro referee will know when the player or coach has had his say, and will know when to walk away. An average one won't. *— Sig Borgia, referee.*

540 He comes into the league with all that fancy stuff and they call it magic. I've been doing it for years and they call it school yard. *— Joe Bryant, San Diego Clippers forward, on Earvin (Magic) Johnson.*

541 He got tired of his dad writing him for money. *— Beano Cook, Pittsburgh sports information director, on why a player had quit school.*

542 Here's a 6-foot-10 guy in sneakers and the lady's asking me, "Profession?" *— Jack McMahon, Cincinnati Royals coach, after taking his center to the hospital.*

543 He's just like any other 7-foot black millionaire who lives next door. *— Alex Hannum, Philadephia 76ers coach, on Wilt Chamberlain.*

544 How fair is it to incarcerate a person who was doing what nearly everyone in the community wanted him to do — namely, winning basketball games? The real hypocrisy is when colleges across the country maintain and establish what amounts to pro teams in the guise of amateur athletics. *— Phillip Baiamonte, District Court judge, imposing a lenient one-year deferred sentence on New Mexico coach Norm Ellenberger for his role in a recruiting scandal.*

545 I ask a player, "Are you happy with this contract?" He'll say, yes, he is. "Fine", I tell him, "I'm happy, too. We're both happy. But I have one provision before we sign this contract. There will not be any renegotiation, because I want you to be aware that if you get hurt, we pay the full contract; and if you have a bad year, we're still obligated to pay. Remember, you have security and peace of mind for two-three years. You have everything. I'm the one taking the big gamble, not you. I only ask one thing. Don't ever ask to renegotiate a term contract with me. Remember, you're the one who asked for it in the first place". — *Arnold (Red) Auerbach, Boston Celtics general manager.*

546 I called time out and told the Catholics they had to go to church tomorrow, and the non-Catholics they should think about God. And play some defense. — *Nick Macarchuk, Canisius basketball coach, when his team was trailing in overtime.*

547 I came in, the fans were looking for another Wilt. But Wilt had his own style and you can't fill his shoes, no way. I could play 10-12 years and get no respect. A lot more people think you're garbage than great. — *Darryl Dawkins, Philadelphia 76ers center, on playing in Wilt Chamberlain's shadow.*

548 I cannot imagine anyplace else on earth that I would rather be at this moment than right here, about to play in the final game of the championship of the world. — *Bill Bradley, New York Knickerbockers forward, before the seventh game of the NBA championships.*

549 I can see why fans don't like to watch pro basketball. I don't either. It's not exciting. — *Larry Bird, Boston Celtics rookie forward.*

550 I can't stand a ballplayer who plays in fear. — *Arnold (Red) Auerbach, Boston Celtics coach.*

551 I consider playing professional basketball as marking time, the most shallow thing in the world. — *Bill Russell, Boston Celtics center.*

552 I discovered as a kid that the way to win was not to have a bunch of guys who could shoot 20-foot jump shots. What we'd do is get five average guys who could shoot layups. Then we'd pass — and win. — *Earvin (Magic) Johnson, Los Angeles Lakers guard.*

553 I dislike the hypocrisy of coaching. They call some guys great coaches, but look how they get the players. One coach in the Southwest Conference reports another for cheating and everyone wants to know who the dirty rat was who turned him in. — *Abe Lemons, Texas basketball coach.*

554 I don't like talking about money. All I know is the Good Lord must have wanted me to have it. — *Larry Bird, Boston Celtics forward.*

555 I don't look for excuses when we lose, and I don't buy excuses when we win. — *Dave Cowens, Boston Celtics center.*

556 I don't think we've been beaten by officials more than five times this season. — *Phil Johnson, Weber State basketball coach, on his 18-5 team.*

557 I'd rather have a lot of talent and little experience than a lot of experience and little talent. — *John Wooden, UCLA basketball coach.*

558 I'd rather play a pinball machine than watch a basketball game today. You score the same number of points. — *Chick Davies, former Duquesne basketball coach.*

559 I'd trade every one of you, except you're so bad no one will have you. — *Charlie Wolf, Detroit Pistons coach, to his players shortly before he was fired.*

560 If a coach starts listening to the fans, he winds up sitting next to them. — *Johnny Kerr, former NBA coach.*

561 If a coach wants to pick up a paper and read what he wants to read, he should take out an ad. It's the sign of a coach slipping when he becomes vindictive to a reporter. — *Al McGuire, announcer.*

562 If God wasn't for the Tar Heels, then why did he make the sky Carolina blue? — *Anonymous, on the University of North Carolina.*

563 If I can keep my team out of jail, we should do all right in the playoffs. — *Al Bianchi, Virginia Squires coach.*

564 If I can miss five minutes, I feel like I'm adding five years to my life. — *Wilt Chamberlain, Philadelphia 76er's center, on Alex Hannum's practices.*

565 If the Cougars have one outstanding trait, it's mediocrity. — *Marv Harshman, Washington State basketball coach.*

566 If we can get a boy one year of college, it's better than no years at all. Once in a while one stays long enough to catch the message, and anything is better than letting them go off the deep end. — *Will Robinson, Pershing basketball coach.*

567 If you always tell the truth, you don't have anything to remember. — *Dick Motta, Chicago Bulls coach, on his candor with the press.*

568 If you're a positive person, you're an automatic motivator. You can get people to do things you don't think they're capable of. — *Cotton Fitzsimmons, Kansas City Kings coach.*

569 If you took a secret poll of the NBA players and asked them, "Are you having fun?" — boy, I think the answers would be very sad. — *Wilt Chamberlain, former Los Angeles Lakers center.*

570 I have a great deal more respect for someone who keeps coming back after losing heartbreaker after heartbreaker than I do for the winner who has everything going for him. Basketball, as you know, is a game of variables. — *Wilt Chamberlain, Los Angeles Lakers center.*

571 I hope they don't find it. — *Buster Brannon, Texas Christian basketball coach, after the ball went under the stands during a 101-55 defeat.*

572 I know it. I'm gonna get in shape as soon as the season's over. — *Wendell Ladner, New York Nets forward, after being told he was fat.*

573 I know now you can't teach a boy to shoot. It's something that comes naturally. You either have the knack or you don't. — *Joe Fulks, former Philadelphia Warrior.*

574 I learned a long time ago that minor surgery is when they do the operation on somebody else, not you. — *Bill Walton, San Diego Clippers center.*

575 I like to judge a trade by seeing which guy reports first. — *Bob Ferry, Washington Bullets general manager.*

576 I love basketball, but I am concerned that the game is too long, the season is too long and the players are too long. — *Jack Dolph, ABA commissioner.*

577 I love long hair and beards and mustaches. Yes, sir. If you want to look like you want to look, dress like you want to dress, act like you want to act, play like you want to play, shoot like you want to shoot, do your own thing, I say, "great". But you're sure as hell not coming to Indiana to play basketball. At Indiana, we're going to do my thing. — *Bobby Knight, Indiana basketball coach.*

578 I'm going to try to come back. I might grow ugly, but I'll never grow old. — *Tom Thacker, Indiana Pacers veteran.*

579 I'm just an average player who can do fantastic things. — *Billy Ray Bates, Portland Trail Blazers guard.*

580 I'm not saying there's no finesse in the pro game; but the college game is mainly finesse, the pro game is mainly brute strength. — *John Wooden, UCLA basketball coach.*

581 I'm the 13th man on this team, and the only difference is that I have veto power over the other 12. — *Alex Hannum, San Diego Rockets coach.*

582 In college a defender can't touch his man. But in the pros, he can damn near beat him to death. — *Tom Henderson, Atlanta Hawks guard, on the difference between professional and college basketball.*

583 I never preach religion to my players, but I won't tolerate profanity. This isn't for moral reasons. Profanity to me symbolizes loss of control — and self discipline is absolutely necessary to winning basketball. — *John Wooden, UCLA basketball coach.*

584 In rebounding, position is the key. No two objects can occupy the same place at the same time. Seventy-five percent of all rebounds are taken below the height of the rim, so timing is important because almost everybody in the NBA can get up high enough to touch the rim. — *Bill Russell, Boston Celtics coach.*

585 Instead of firing the coach, we've fired the team. — *Ned Doyle, Miami Floridians owner, after trading 10 of his 11 players.*

586 I recruited Jimmy to pave Marquette's way to the big time. He's got every right to leave now and do the same for himself. — *Al McGuire, Marquette basketball coach, on his star junior center Jim Chones turning professional.*

587 I resent the hell out of the question. I don't take any honor or any dignity in being the first black anything anywhere because I think it implies that I am the first one who had the ability or the intelligence, and I find it extremely offensive. — *John Thompson, Georgetown basketball coach, asked about being the first black coach in the NCAA final four.*

588 I sight down my nose to shoot, and now my nose isn't straight since I broke it. That's why my shooting has been off. — *Barrie Haynie, Centenary basketball player, on his jump shot.*

589 I should have gotten an idea what it would be like back in December when my engagement was announced on the sports page. — *Pam Hale, wife of basketball player Rick Barry.*

590 I tell them I don't know where they're supposed to go. — *Fred Lewis, Syracuse basketball coach on his free-lance press.*

591 It is an admission that you are dealing with inferior players who can't do anything but throw up long shots. — *Eddie Gottlieb, NBA rules committeeman, on the ABA's three-point shot.*

592 I think back and remember how I used to enjoy playing the game, itself, so much. It was fun for me and everyone in college. I loved it. But money changes the game. Once everybody is out trying to get as much money as he can, it becomes different. All the fun goes out of it. And, somehow, it never really seems the same again. — *Curtis Rowe, former UCLA Bruins and Boston Celtics forward.*

593 I think I've got the best job in America. If I wasn't doing this for a living, I'd probably be playing a couple nights a week at the "Y" someplace and I'd end up with all these bumps and bruises for free. — *Julius Erving, Philadelphia 76ers forward.*

594 I tried to treat them like men — and some of them weren't. — *Bill Russell, former Seatle Supersonics coach, on his players.*

595 It's a lot like shaving; if you don't do it everyday, you're a bum. — *Bob Boyd, Southern California basketball coach, on recruiting.*

596 It's better to go too far with a boy than not far enough. — *John Wooden, UCLA basketball coach.*

597 It's courage and character that make the difference between players and great players, between great surgeons and ones who bury their mistakes. — *Pete Carril, Princeton basketball coach.*

598 It's just one more referee to yell at. — *Norm Stewart, Missouri basketball coach, on using three officials.*

599 It's not how high you jump but how much space you take up when you get up there. — *Dave Cowens, Boston Celtics center, on rebounding.*

600 It's the non-athlete who's afraid of discipline. Athletes want it and need it. Time has changed the game of basketball, but the basics are the same. We have to emphasize that in this day of slam dunks and hero worship and entertainers. — *Bill Foster, Duke basketball coach.*

601 It's what I call a sieve. I don't think it's going to catch on, though. — *Abe Lemons, Oklahoma City basketball coach, on his team's defense.*

602 I've never seen an athlete, including myself, who I think should be lionized. There are very few athletes I know whom I would want my kids to be like. — *Bill Russell, Seattle Supersonics coach.*

603 I want a team that is sound; and so strong that if the referee cheats we'll win, and if we go south we'll win, and if we play UCLA at UCLA we'll win. Winning is the thing. If it wasn't, they wouldn't keep score. — *Will Robinson, Illinois State basketball coach.*

604 Let's play a home-and-home series, but let's play both at your place. — *Abe Lemons, Oklahoma City basketball coach, speaking to the Miami, Florida coach.*

605 Life is good. But basketball is better. — *Lou Carnesecca, St. John's basketball coach.*

606 Losing a basketball game isn't the greatest tragedy imaginable. I'm sorry we lost, but we've got to be men. — *Ray Meyer, DePaul basketball coach, after an unexpected loss in the NCAA tournament.*

607 A lot of coaches are interested in upgrading their schedules. I'd rather schedule teams I can beat so I can improve my record and keep my job. — *Bob LeGrand, Arlington basketball coach.*

608 A lot of coaches won't agree with me, but kids do go to college for financial security; and if they get a chance at a good contract, they should take it. To me, it's like a student majoring in business administration having a chance to leave school and become a vice-president at General Motors. — *Dean Smith, North Carolina basketball coach, on undergraduates signing professional contracts.*

609 A man's reach should exceed his grasp. — *Willis Reed, New York Knickerbockers center.*

610 Mentally, it kills you. Even if you win, you can't enjoy it while you're out on the court. — *Jim McMillian, Buffalo Braves forward, on the NBA playoffs.*

611 More games are won during the months of recruiting than during the weeks of the season. — *Jack Gardner, Utah basketball coach.*

612 Most kids who make it big in life, or in the pros, are winners by the time they leave high school. I don't say a man can't change and become a winner later; but it's tougher then. I found the really good ones win early and never lose the habit. I can't explain it, but if kids like that go into the pros, they eventually wind up ... a winner. — *Willis Reed, New York Knickerbockers center.*

613 My teammates tell me I have white man's disease. — *Phil Ford, North Carolina guard, admitting he can't dunk.*

614 My wife asked me why we didn't have rooms like this in our house and I told her because I'm only an owner. — *Richard Bloch, Phoenix Suns owner, after looking at Wilt Chamberlain's $1.5 million house.*

615 No coach is going to make a great shooter out of an ordinary one. But the average boy can learn to be a fine defensive player. — *Henry Iba, Oklahoma State basketball coach.*

616 No man can coach his buddies. — *Frank McGuire, Philadelphia 76ers coach.*

617 No matter how much money you make, if you're dumb, somebody's going to take it away from you. So get an education. — *Leroy Ellis, Philadelphia 76ers center.*

618 Officiating is the only occupation in the world where the highest accolade is silence. — *Dolly King, referee.*

619 Officiating should be developed into a career, with a college degree required. — *Press Maravich, Louisiana State basketball coach.*

620 One-third of the teams in Division I are going to tournaments when the season's over. I got a hunch a lot of coaches that don't go will be fired. — *Jerry Lyne, Loyola of Chicago basketball coach.*

621 The only coaching secrets left in the game are in recruiting. — *Al McGuire, Marquette basketball coach.*

622 The only place a ball like that belongs is on the end of a seal's nose. — *Alex Hannum, Oakland Oaks coach, on the ABA's red, white and blue ball.*

623 The only thing in this country that blacks really dominate, except for poverty, is basketball. — *Al McGuire, Marquette basketball coach.*

624 The only time I use chalk is to throw it. — *Butch van Breda Kolff, Princeton basketball coach.*

625 The only time they called a foul was when somebody's nose bled. — *Abe Lemons, Oklahoma City basketball coach, after a rough game.*

626 The opera isn't over till the fat lady sings. — *Dick Motta, Washington Bullets coach.*

627 Our players are all NBA players but there is some question whether they should all be on the same team. — *Del Harris, Houston Rockets coach.*

628 People keep saying we are the worst defensive team in the league. Actually, we are second — our opponents are the worst. — *Doug Moe, Denver Nuggets coach, on the 126.5 scoring and 126 point defensive average.*

629 People like me. — *Dennis Awtrey, Seattle Supersonics center, on being traded six times in eight years.*

630 People promised me things. They said I'd get a million dollars. I figured I'd have the big home and all the rest, you know, like everyone else. — *Raymond Lewis, former Philadelphia 76ers guard, on quitting school to join the NBA.*

631 People say I owe the public this and I owe the public that. What I owe the public is the best performance I can give, period. — *Bill Russell, Boston Celtics center.*

632 People see what they want to see, and most pro basketball fans have limited vision after they get past the scoring column. They look to see how many points a player gets and that is how they judge him. It makes no sense, but it's true. — *K.C. Jones, Washington Bullets coach.*

633 Players have to know that when they sign a contract, it means they are saying that for this amount, I will give 100 percent of my body. My job will be to tell them when they are giving 85 percent and that they owe me 15. — *Willis Reed, New York Knickerbockers coach.*

634 The player today in the pro game — or even in college and high school — is worried about himself and not the team. No pro team really has a team spirit. The pro says to himself, "I've got to play or I'll lose my value". I guess that's a realistic outlook; but it's not mine. — *Butch van Breda Kolff, Detroit Pistons coach, at his resignation.*

635 Playgrounds are the best place to learn the game, because if you lose, you sit down. — *Gary Williams, American basketball coach.*

636 Playing in the NBA isn't a beauty contest. They're all ugly. — *Al Menendez, New Jersey Nets scout.*

637 Playing sports is orgasmic, instinctive. If you're going to be a good athlete, you cannot think. — *Phil Jackson, New York Knickerbockers forward.*

638 The primary job of a coach is to make sure his team doesn't lose games it should win. — *Earl Lloyd, Detroit Pistons coach.*

639 Red Auerbach makes mistakes, the entire Boston team makes mistakes, but they can get away with it because they have the world's largest eraser in Bill Russell. — *Pepper Wilson, Cincinnati Royals general manager, on the Boston Celtics.*

640 Run fast, but don't hurry. — *John Wooden, UCLA basketball coach, on how to execute a fast break.*

641 The season was one of the great experiences for the city, for the team brought people from all walks of life together. — *Walter Washington, former District of Columbia mayor, on the Washington Bullets' championship.*

642 Sometimes I get up and cuss and swear and feel like grabbing one of the

guys and smacking him. Then I say, "What the hell am I doing?" These
are grown men out there, half-naked, running up and down throwing a ball
around, getting enormous amounts of money for doing it—and I'm getting
mad. —*Bill Russell, Seattle Supersonics coach.*

643   Some year I'm going to write our book. And it's going to say, "I wish I
        had never recruited this player. He has eaten $5,000 worth of groceries
and has cost us $10,000 overall, and he's scored one point. He's a dog." —*Abe
Lemons, Texas basketball coach, on press guides.*

644   Son, looks to me like you're spending too much time on one subject.
        —*Shelby Metcalf, Texas A & M basketball coach, after seeing a player's
4 F and 1 D report card.*

645   So what if they're taller? We'll play big. —*George Ireland, Loyola of
        Chicago basketball coach.*

646   Statistics are the cancer of basketball. —*Al McGuire, Marquette basket-
        ball coach.*

647   Success is never final. Failure is never fatal. It's courage that counts.
        —*John Wooden, former UCLA basketball coach.*

648   Success is the best builder of character. —*Adolph Rupp, former Ken-
        tucky basketball coach.*

649   The sun don't shine on the same dog's butt every day. —*Babe McCarthy,
        Memphis Pros coach, on the team's losing streak.*

650   A team that combines the talent of Minnesota and Houston, the en-
        thusiasm of North Carolina and a couple of Notre Dame referees.
—*Marv Harshman, Washington basketball coach, on the ingredients needed
to defeat UCLA.*

651   There is a truth I understand now. When everything is said and done,
        all I will be is the answer to a trivia question. —*George McGinnis, former
Indiana Pacers forward, on retiring at age 32.*

652   There's nobody in the world knows so much as a damn sophomore.
        —*Peck Hickman, Louisville basketball coach.*

653   There's no easier way to make a living than a pro athlete. Then, all of a
        sudden, you wake up and realize you have to go to work for a living.
—*Bob Pettit, former St. Louis Hawks center.*

654   These days you don't dictate to an athlete what he must do. They do
        what they darn please. You ask a guy to give you five minutes of his

time to talk to a newspaperman and the player will tell you to get lost. I tell you, they make so much money these days and get so independent they're impossible in many cases. — *Hymie Perlo, Baltimore Bullets executive.*

655 They go on and on. It's like a guy telling a bad joke for 15 minutes. — *Tom Heinson, Boston Celtics coach, on the NBA playoffs.*

656 This is as thrilling as artificial insemination. — *Bill Currie, radio announcer, during a stall.*

657 This is bad for team morale. — *Harvey Murphy, North Carolina-Charlotte basketball coach, when 6 of his 11 players were ruled academically ineligible.*

658 This is not the non-contact sport they say it is ... I have to be aggressive to earn a living. I don't want to be involved in anything like this, but asking how to get violence out of pro basketball is like asking how to get it out of society. — *Kermit Washington, Los Angeles Lakers forward, on his 60 day suspension for punching Rudy Tomjanovich.*

659 This is one of the best teams I've ever had — academically. — *Lou Rossini, Columbia basketball coach.*

660 This team isn't worth a damn, but it just doesn't know it. — *Adolph Rupp, Kentucky basketball coach.*

661 This year I had a kid who wanted to come out and rest. I told him to get out there and play. Rest on the floor. How can a guy get tired? An apache can run down a horse. So how can a person get tired playing basketball? Getting tired is inside of you. — *Abe Lemons, Texas basketball coach.*

662 This year we plan to run and shoot. Next season we hope to run and score. — *Billy Tubbs, Oklahoma basketball coach.*

663 The toughest thing in the National Basketball Association is to get them to want it ... want the victory ... want the execution ... as badly as you do. — *Hubie Brown, Atlanta Hawks coach.*

664 The trouble with athletes today is that they are great at rationalizing. Too many won't stand up and take the blame and admit they didn't produce. When one does, you have a rare man. — *Hubie Brown, Atlanta Hawks coach.*

665 The trouble with officials is, they just don't care who wins. — *Tommy Canterbury, Centenary basketball coach, on officials after losing a game.*

666 Until I got good at basketball ... there was nothing about me that I liked. There wasn't a thing that I could be proud of. — *Connie Hawkins, Phoenix Sun forward.*

667   War is hell, but expansion is worse. — *Bill Fitch, Cleveland Cavaliers coach.*

668   The way defenses are operating these days, the other team starts picking you up when you walk out of the hotel lobby. — *Doc Hayes, Southern Methodist basketball coach.*

669   We are not going to play them; they are going to play us. — *Henry Iba, Oklahoma State basketball coach.*

670   We can't go around apologizing because we're professional basketball players. We've got to have pride — pride in ourselves and in our teams and in our league. — *Bob Cousy, Boston Celtics guard.*

671   We just got buzzards luck. Nothing will die and we can't kill nothing. — *Jack Crawford, San Francisco basketball player, during a losing streak.*

672   We'll jump off that bridge when we come to it. — *Bill Fitch, Cleveland Cavaliers coach, on his last place team.*

673   We lost some mighty good boys from last year because of paroles, but, crime being what it is, we've picked up some good ones since then, too. — *Joe Kirkpatrick, Oklahoma State Penitentiary basketball coach.*

674   Wendell doesn't know the meaning of the word fear, but then he doesn't know the meaning of most words. — *Babe McCarthy, Kentucky Colonel coach, on forward Wendell Ladner.*

675   We've got a great bunch of backup players. We'd make somebody a hell of a farm club. — *Bill Fitch, Cleveland Cavaliers coach.*

676   We've got too many boy scouts on this team and not enough killers. — *Dick Vitale, Detroit Pistons coach.*

677   What difference does it make if a guy sleeps 11 p.m. to 9 a.m. or 2 a.m. to noon? If he gets his rest, he gets his rest. — *Bob Gaillard, San Francisco basketball coach, on curfews.*

678   When I was in high school and college, I thought the guys in the NBA always cooled it out until the fourth quarter. It was almost as if they didn't care. Well, it's true. — *Isiah Thomas, Detroit Pistons rookie guard.*

679   When my brothers wouldn't let me play with them, I promised myself

I would get good enough so they'd have to let my play. — *Oscar Robertson, Cincinnati Royals guard.*

680   When people are used to winning, they put out a little more. — *Arnold (Red) Auerbach, Boston Celtics coach.*

681   When the game is on Ash Wednesday and the ref shows up with a smudge on his forehead, I know I'm in trouble. — *Jack McCloskey, Wake Forest basketball coach, after losing to St. Joseph's.*

682   When we play a bad game, it's like desecrating the flag. — *Dennis Awtrey, Philadelphia 76ers center, on their red, white and blue uniforms.*

683   When you have a curfew, it's always your star who gets caught. — *Abe Lemons, Oklahoma City basketball coach, on why he doesn't set a curfew.*

684   When you're through playing, when you're older, you go back to your friends. — *Dave DeBusschere, former New York Knickerbockers forward.*

685   Winning makes everyone a star. — *Lenny Wilkins, Seattle Supersonics coach.*

686   This world is made up of Davids. I am a Goliath. And nobody roots for Goliath. — *Wilt Chamberlain, former NBA center.*

687   Yes, the fact that he's white. — *Al Attles, Golden State Warriors coach, on whether anything about Bill Walton surprised him.*

688   You can have all the talent in the world, but if you're not interested in making full use of that talent, victory is unlikely. — *George Mikan, Minneapolis Lakers center.*

689   You can teach anything if you believe in it and you can understand it. — *Ralph Miller, Iowa basketball coach.*

690   You can only wear one suit at a time, drive one car and eat just three meals a day. What do I need with a million dollars? — *David Thompson, North Carolina State forward, rejecting a professional contract after his junior year.*

691   You can win and still not succeed, still not achieve what you should. And you can lose without really failing at all. — *Bobby Knight, Indiana basketball coach.*

692   You can't win an NBA title in one game unless it's the last game. But you can lose it in one game. — *John Bassett, attorney, after San Diego Clippers Bill Walton injured his foot.*

693 You don't get tired when you're playing for a national championship. — *Lefty Driesell, Maryland basketball coach.*

694 You don't try to handle basketball players. You handle horses and animals. — *Wilt Chamberlain, San Diego Conquistadors coach, on his new duties.*

695 Young man, you have the question backwards. — *Bill Russell, former Boston Celtics center, asked how he would fare against Kareem Abdul-Jabbar.*

Billiards *see* Pool

Boxing

696 Ain't but one champion, just like there ain't but one President of the United States. — *Muhammad Ali, heavyweight champion, after being stripped of his title.*

697 Always go with the banger. — *Anonymous.*

698 America wasn't built on going to church; it was built on violence. I express America in the ring. — *Ron Lyle, heavyweight boxer.*

699 Anybody who can be hit, can be whipped. — *John Kilbane, featherweight champion.*

700 Anyone who weighs over 200 pounds can punch — I don't care if it's a broad. — *Angelo Dundee, boxing manager.*

701 The bigger they come, the harder they fall. — *Bob Fitzsimmons, heavyweight champion.*

702 Blood is like champagne to a fighter. — *Al Lacy, boxing trainer.*

703 Boxing is a hard way to make an easy dollar. — *Anonymous.*

704   Boxing is sort of like jazz. The better it is, the less amount of people can appreciate it. — *George Foreman, heavyweight champion.*

705   Boxing is the one opportunity for the low man on the ethnic totem pole. It is a short cut to money, prestige, status, power. — *Cus D'Amato, boxing manager.*

706   A boxing match is like a cowboy movie — there's got to be the good guys and there's got to be the bad guys. — *Sonny Liston, heavyweight champion.*

707   Boxing might have been going on in New York right now if the men who had charge of the clubs had handled it with credit. They made the mistake by not stopping contests when they became brutal, or when it was manifest to all that one of the contestants had no possible chance of winning. — *Theodore Roosevelt, Vice-President of the United States in 1901.*

708   The boxing world needs changes, and the first thing it needs is more white boxers. And the only way you're going to get white boxers is for the nation to have a major depression. I know that's a horrible thing to say, but it's true. — *Jerry Quarry, heavyweight.*

709   The dumbest question I was ever asked by a sportswriter was whether I hit harder with red or white gloves. As a matter of fact, I hit harder with red. — *Frank Crawford, boxer.*

710   Everybody wants a piece of the cake, but my cake has no slices. — *Ingemar Johansson, heavyweight champion.*

711   Everybody wants to go to heaven, but nobody wants to die. — *Joe Louis, former heavyweight champion.*

712   A fellow with a punch has a short cut to victory. — *Charlie Goldman, boxing trainer.*

713   A fighter has to know fear. — *Cus D'Amato, boxing trainer.*

714   A fighter who thinks about losing is a born loser. — *Joe Frazier, heavyweight champion.*

715   Fighting is hard. But there are harder things. — *Costenito Gonzalez, boxer.*

716   First your legs go. Then you lose your reflexes. Then you lose your friends. — *Willie Pep, former featherweight champion, on aging boxers.*

717   Float like a butterfly, sting like a bee. — *Muhammad Ali, heavyweight champion.*

718 From now on, he fights his wife. — *Alex Koskowitz, boxing manager, after heavyweight Doug Jones was KO'd.*

719 God is always on the side of the puncher. — *George Foreman, heavyweight champion.*

720 The golden age of prizefighting was the age of bad food, bad air, bad sanitation and no sunlight. — *Lou Stillman, boxing trainer.*

721 Hail the conquering hero comes, surrounded by a bunch of bums. — *George Phair, writer, on Jack Dempsey and his entourage.*

722 A heavyweight champion shouldn't think so much about money. A champion should help the boxing game by fighting often. When he doesn't fight often, it hurts boxing, because he's the man at the top, the one everyone looks up to. When he's idle, boxing's idle. — *Joe Louis, former heavyweight champion.*

723 He can run, but he can't hide. — *Joe Louis, heavyweight champion, on challenger Billy Conn.*

724 He isn't a puncher. He just hit me so many times I didn't know where I was. — *Brian London, heavyweight, after fighting Muhammad Ali.*

725 He said he'd bring home the bacon, and the honey boy has gone and done it. — *"Tiny" Johnson, mother of Jack Johnson, after Jack defeated Jim Jeffries for the heavyweight title.*

726 He's a credit to his race — the human race. — *Jimmy Cannon, writer, on heavyweight champion Joe Louis.*

727 He's everything a heavyweight champion should be — except busy. — *Rocky Marciano, former heavyweight champion, on Floyd Patterson.*

728 He's the best negative fighter around. He's never there and he's always ready to run. — *Gil Clancy, boxing manager, on boxer Jimmy Archer.*

729 He was the perfect combination — showman, fighter and rat. — *Jackie McCoy, boxing manager, on lightweight Art Aragon.*

730 He was as good as a fighter can be without being a hell of a fighter. — *A.J. Liebling, writer, on welterweight Billy Graham in "The Sweet Science".*

731 Hey, Ma, your bad boy done it. I told you somebody up there likes me. — *Rocky Graziano, middleweight champion, after defeating Tony Zale for the title.*

732   I ain't got no quarrel with them Viet Congs. — *Muhammad Ali, heavyweight champion, refusing induction into the U.S. Army.*

733   I am the best. I just haven't played yet. — *Muhammad Ali, heavyweight champion, on playing golf.*

734   I am the greatest. — *Muhammad Ali, heavyweight champion.*

735   I can lick any man in the house. — *John L. Sullivan, heavyweight boxer.*

736   I consider myself blessed. I consider you blessed. We've all been blessed with God-given talents. Mine just happens to be beating people up. — *Ray Leonard, welterweight champion.*

737   I don't believe it. Start counting ten over him and he'll get up. — *Wilson Mizner, boxing manager, when he heard of boxer Stanley Ketchel's death.*

738   I don't care what religion he is. If he doesn't get a moving, he's gonna lose the fight. — *Gil Clancy, announcer, when told a boxer was a vegetarian.*

739   I don't like money, actually, but it quiets my nerves. — *Joe Louis, heavyweight champion.*

740   I don't mind if he beats my husband, as long as he leaves me a little bit. — *Veronica London, wife of heavyweight Brian London, before his match with Muhammad Ali.*

741   I really don't fight to win, I fight to survive. — *Jimmy Young, heavyweight.*

742   I don't want to be a millionaire. I just want to be able to live like one. — *Michael Dokes, heavyweight.*

743   If a corner gets rattled, it's a cinch the fighter will too. — *Eddie Futch, boxing manager.*

744   If a kid says he wants to be a fighter, you know right away he isn't smart. — *Anonymous.*

745   If I lose, then I still will have the most thrilling thing of all — the money. — *Floyd Patterson, former heavyweight champion, before a rematch with Ingemar Johannson.*

746   If my fans think I can do everything I say I can do, then they're crazier than I am. — *Muhammad Ali, heavyweight champion in 1962.*

747 If there's anything I hate, it's a bully. — *Jack Dempsey, heavyweight champion.*

748 If you kill the body, then the head must die. — *Doc Moore, boxing trainer.*

749 I had 27 sinus operations, and now they say you shouldn't have any. That's how they found out. — *Jack Hurley, boxing manager.*

750 I have fought once too often. — *John L. Sullivan, former heavyweight champion, after his defeat by James Corbett.*

751 I have no debts, also none of the more than $1 million I made as a fighter. — *Ezzard Charles, former heavyweight champion, on his $100-per-week job as a driver's license examiner.*

752 I have proven to be superior in speed, skill, looks and brains to every other heavyweight in the world. I came out with no scratches. I'm well invested. I beat boxing. Boxing didn't beat me. — *Muhammad Ali, former heavyweight champion.*

753 I'll come out smokin'. — *Joe Frazier, heavyweight boxer, on how he would fight Jimmy Ellis for the title.*

754 I'll moider de bum. — *Tony Galento, heavyweight boxer, asked what he thought of William Shakespeare.*

755 I love boxing. I loved every minute of it, every round in the gym, every skip of the rope and every foot on the road. The fights were the dessert. — *Carmen Basilio, former welterweight champion.*

756 I love everybody in the whole world, but I don't trust nobody. — *Leon Spinks, heavyweight champion.*

757 I'm a realist. You don't enter a Volkswagen at Indy unless you know a helluva shortcut. — *Darlene Stander, wife of heavyweight Ron Stander, when asked of her opinion of Ron's TKO by champion Joe Frazier.*

758 I'm a trainer, not a magician. If a fighter doesn't have it, only God can help him. — *Eddie Futch, boxing trainer.*

759 I'm gonna have to be killed before I lose and I ain't going to die easy. — *Muhammad Ali, heavyweight champion.*

760 In any championship fight, the guy only holds the title until the bell rings. — *Gil Clancy, boxing manager.*

761 In this game, you have to be a finisher. I call it "finishing", and you don't learn it in Miss Hewitt's school for young ladies. — *Archie Moore, former light heavyweight champion.*

762 I owe everything I have to boxing. I owe the milkman, the grocer, the newspaper boy, the.... — *Art Aragon, former lightweight boxer.*

763 I realize that if I am ever to enjoy the easy life, it must come through boxing. — *Curtis Cokes, welterweight boxer.*

764 I say get an education. Become an electrician, a mechanic, a doctor, a lawyer — anything but a fighter. In this trade, it's the managers who make the money and last the longest. I know if I ever become the father of a boy, he won't be a prizefighter. — *Muhammad Ali, former heavyweight champion.*

765 It doesn't matter who the heavyweight champion fights or where, just so he fights. — *Chris Dundee, boxing promoter.*

766 I told him, "How can I live off 25 percent of nothing?" — *Jim Wicks, boxing manager of Henry Cooper, on Cooper's statement he would fight Cassius Clay for nothing.*

767 It's a funny business, isn't it — hitting people in the head? — *Roy Harris, heavyweight boxer.*

768 It takes a lot of man in heart and mind to challenge for the title. — *Joe Frazier, heavyweight champion.*

769 It will take dynamite to get me to 175 pounds. — *Archie Moore, light-heavyweight champion, on losing 25 pounds to make weight.*

770 I wanted to kill him. I got nothing against him, he's a nice guy. But I wanted to kill him. — *Rocky Graziano, middleweight champion, asked how he felt when he had Tony Zale in the corner.*

771 I want to develop real sportsmen, and not just bums thirsting for knockouts. — *Zsigmond Adler, Hungarian boxing coach, on his retirement.*

772 I want to leave boxing with a little bit of looks and the ability to talk. — *Jerry Quarry, heavyweight boxer.*

773 I was down, but I wasn't out. — *Gene Tunney, heavyweight champion, on his "long-count" fight with Jack Dempsey.*

774 I wasn't even out of the house. — *Willie Pep, former featherweight champion, on a report stating he had died.*

775 Let me tell you about boxing. It's the most treacherous, dirtiest, vicious, cheatingest game in the world.... That's the nature of the business. —*Paddy Flood, boxing promoter.*

776 Liston has a lot of good qualities. It's his bad qualities that are not so good. —*George Katz, boxing manager of Sonny Liston.*

777 Lord, don't let me kill this guy. Just let me beat him up and get the hell out of here. —*Larry Holmes, heavyweight champion, on the prayer he says in the ring.*

778 May the superior adversary emerge victorious. —*Harry Balogh, boxing announcer.*

779 The most exciting moment (in sports) is still the heavyweight championship fight. You get caught up in the scary anticipation of the whole goddamn thing. Those two men are half naked and hitting one another. And every instinct is basic, and every reaction is basic, and the brutality is basic. The human animal is captured by it. You wonder which man is going to give way to fear. —*Howard Cosell, announcer.*

780 Never underestimate a puncher. —*Whitey Bimstein, boxing trainer.*

781 99 and 45/100 percent of all boxers I have known are great people. —*Don Dunphy, boxing announcer.*

782 Nobody owes anybody a living, but everybody is entitled to a chance. —*Jack Dempsey, former heavyweight champion.*

783 No, his manager did. —*Sonny Liston, heavyweight boxer, asked if an opponent "had heart" during a brutal beating.*

784 No mas, no mas. —*Roberto Duran, former welterweight champion, quitting his title fight with Sugar Ray Leonard.*

785 Not yet, but I'd like to say right now that if I meet an accidental death, it wouldn't be accidental. —*Fraser Scott, middleweight boxer, asked if he had any contacts with criminal figures.*

786 One day you are the champ and your friends say, "No one in the world can beat you champ." Then you are no longer the champ and you are all alone. —*Sonny Liston, former heavyweight champion.*

787 Power thrills, but speed kills. —*Michael Dokes, heavyweight boxer.*

788 A professional fighter is not supposed to show the effect of a punch. —*Jose Torres, light heavyweight boxer.*

789 The public likes a fearless slugger, but that won't pay your hospital bills. — *Willie Pep, former featherweight champion.*

790 The punch that knocks a man out is the punch that he doesn't see. Have you ever seen the pea in the shell game? The man who works the game must have the ability to direct attention to the wrong area. That's what happens in boxing. — *Cus D'Amato, boxing manager.*

791 Punch up, punch down, what the hell's the difference? — *Tony Galento, heavyweight boxer, on his short stature.*

792 Putting a fighter in the business world is like putting silk stockings on a pig. — *Jack Hurley, boxing manager.*

793 The ring is absolutely safe. In my opinion, there is nothing safer than two fighters boxing in a ring. If a fighter was hit as often as the public thinks, they never would have to abolish boxing. All the fighters would quit fighting. — *Cus D'Amato, boxing manager.*

794 A shot to the jaw can kill someone. Death may deter some kids, but it won't have any effect on anyone who really wants to be in boxing. To think you can have boxing with no fatalities is not reality. — *John Condon, Madison Square Garden vice-president.*

795 A small mishap, a false movement, and the pain will immediately re-appear, the place of injury being forever tender. — *Georges Carpentier, French heavyweight boxer, on the seriousness of a hand injury to a boxer.*

796 Sometimes I feel I'd like to give my memory a knockout and really enjoy life. — *Jack Dempsey, heavyweight champion.*

797 A sportswriter looks up in the sky and then asks you, "Is the sun shining?" — *Sonny Liston, heavyweight champion.*

798 Thank God the reporters weren't up there asking the questions. Then we would have been in trouble. — *Garland Cherry, lawyer, on being the first witness in a 1964 Senate hearing on boxing.*

799 That's a very good sign. It means you're getting your second wind. — *Angelo Dundee, boxing manager, to a slumping fighter complaining of leg weariness.*

800 That's like God asking a man how long he wants to live. — *Sonny Liston, heavyweight champion, asked how long he wanted to keep the title.*

801 There are millions of trainers, but very few teachers. — *Doc Moore, boxing trainer.*

802 There are three sides to every story. My side, the commission's side, and the truth. — *Jack Begun, boxing manager, after being denied a license.*

803 There are two honest managers in boxing. The one is Jack Hurley, and I can't remember the name of the other. — *Damon Runyon, writer.*

804 They cut him four ways — up, down, deep and often. — *Mike DeJohn, heavyweight boxer, on Sonny Liston's managers.*

805 They say what a smart fighter I was. I couldn't have been. I had a manager for two years who fed me nothing but doughnuts and black coffee — and had me loving it. — *Willie Pep, former featherweight champion.*

806 They should take all southpaws and drop them in the river. — *Joe Brown, lightweight champion.*

807 This business of being a champion is a continual game of comparisons. I think of what I was before I knocked out Willard in Toledo and speculate what I'll be after somebody knocks me out somewhere else. They call you a bum before you get to be champion. They call you a bum after somebody slaps you out of the title. And even while you're a champion, you're called a bum. — *Jack Dempsey, heavyweight champion.*

808 This will surprise some people because I was at it for so long, but the truth of the matter is that I hated boxing. It is a cruel, vicious sport — nothing more than two people trying to kill each other — and the more vicious it gets, the more people like it. I'm not an animal. Maybe that's why I didn't become champion. — *Jerry Quarry, heavyweight boxer.*

809 The title is borrowed from the people and must be given back. I plan to take advantage of it while I can treat everybody good, and when it's time to give it up, I'll do so, smiling. — *George Foreman, heavyweight champion.*

810 To see a man beaten not by a better opponent but by himself is a tragedy. — *Cus D'Amato, boxing manager.*

811 We're fighting for only one thing — money. — *Sid Flaherty, boxing manager of Bobo Olson.*

812 We're going to win, because we're on God's side. — *Joe Louis, heavyweight champion, on World War II.*

813 We were so poor every Christmas eve my old man would go outside and shoot his gun, then come in and tell us kids Santa Claus had committed suicide. — *Jake LaMotta, former middleweight champion, on his poor childhood.*

814   We wuz robbed. — *Joe Jacobs, boxing trainer, when Max Schmeling lost a decision to Jack Sharkey.*

815   When I win a fight, it's we won it. When I lose a fight, I lost it. — *Willie Pastrano, light heavyweight boxer.*

816   When you think of a champion, you think of a man fighting in a ring. But there is more, a whole lot more. — *Mike Rossman, light heavyweight champion.*

817   You cannot close your eyes to the fact that it is the wallop that wins. — *Jimmy Wilde, flyweight champion.*

818   You don't know what it is to walk down the street and everybody out there waves at you. — *Al Massey, boxer, on training in Philadelphia.*

819   You know, I never liked fighting, although I guess I owe everything to the ring. — *Ray Robinson, former middleweight champion, on his retirement.*

820   You're damned right I know where I am; I'm in Madison Square Garden getting beaten up. — *Willie Pastrano, former light heavyweight champion asked if he knew where he was after a knock down by Jose Torres.*

Bridge

821   If you regularly lose, you are not the unluckiest player at the table; he is your partner. — *Edward Meyer, English bridge expert.*

822   You win by the other man's mistakes, not by your own brilliance. — *Edward Meyer, English bridge expert.*

Chess

823   The American people as a whole now at least will recognize chess as something played by people and not just wood being pushed around.

—George Kolianowski, American chess grandmaster, after Bobby Fischer won the world championship.

824   Chess is like war on a board. The object is to crush the other man's mind. *—Bobby Fischer, chess champion.*

825   Everything. *—Bobby Fischer, chess champion, asked what chess meant to him.*

826   If I lose, I won't be upset, because I'll know it was a fluke. *—Bobby Fischer, chess player, asked how he would react if he lost the championship match.*

827   In a world where chess is life, the champion is God and God gets what he wants. *—Bobby Fischer, chess champion, on why he refuses to back down from demands.*

828   The mistakes are all there waiting to be made. *—Savielly Tartakower, chess grandmaster, on chess.*

Crew

829   Clemson will never subsidize a sport where a man sits on his tail and goes backward. *—Frank Howard, Clemson athletic director, on why Clemson would not subsidize crew.*

830   Crew is a wonderful tradition at Wisconsin, but we can no longer afford $40,000 worth of tradition. *—Elroy Hirsch, Wisconsin athletic director, on why crew was dropped.*

Football

831   About all that losing gracefully can teach a boy is how to lose. *—James Kelly, Swarthmore football coach.*

832   Academic survival. *—Glenn Cameron, Cincinnati Bengals linebacker, asked his major in college.*

833 All coaches who lead their teams in prayer before games should be forced to attend church once a week. The Good Lord has more to do than worry about the outcome of a football game. — *Duffy Daugherty, former Michigan State football coach.*

834 All I want is 100 percent and a willing disregard for the consequences. — *Red Hickey, San Francisco 49ers coach.*

835 All that spectators get out of the game now is fresh air, the comical articles in his program, the sight of 22 young men rushing about in mysterious formations, and whatever he brought in his flask. — *Robert Benchley, writer.*

836 Alums don't get you fired. They just drive you crazy. The players get you fired. — *Pepper Rodgers, Georgia Tech football coach.*

837 Always have a plan and believe in it. I tell my coaches not to compromise. Nothing good happens by accident. — *Chuck Knox, Los Angeles Rams coach.*

838 The amount of hate I get is directly proportionate to the times we beat the point spread. We beat the spread the last four games last year. I was a hero. I got four letters: "Helluva program you got going — keep it up." In those four games we had three losses and a tie. — *Lee Corso, Indiana football coach.*

839 Anger doesn't win football games. — *Gary Beban, UCLA quarterback.*

840 An angry football team is better than a confident one. — *Pepper Rodgers, UCLA football coach.*

841 Anybody can be normal. It takes a rare individual to be really sick. — *Bob Blanchard, North Carolina State lineman.*

842 Anybody can play offense but it takes a man to play defense. — *Bud Wilkinson, Oklahoma football coach.*

843 An athlete who does not graduate is grossly underpaid as an entertainer. One who graduates is overpaid. — *Joe Paterno, Penn State football coach.*

844 Anyone who tells me, "Don't worry that you lost, you played a good game anyway," I just hate. — *Woody Hayes, Ohio State football coach.*

845 Any time a team thinks beyond its next game, the whole season can be ruined. — *Bob Devaney, Nebraska football coach.*

846 As long as I pay for your room, board, tuition and fees, you're not like other students. I gave you a free ride. The moment I don't pay for a thing you'll be like the others. — *Barry Switzer, Oklahoma football coach, on charges he dominates his players' lives.*

847 As the season progresses I get lighter, faster and more afraid. — *Jerry Levias, Houston Oiler receiver.*

848 Athletics is just about the last place left where discipline is taught. — *Gene Stalling, Texas A & M football coach.*

849 At San Diego State, we had a player who wore a feather in his helmet at practice. Another guy used to practice with a stocking over his face. I don't care if they want to paste Snoopy on their helmets. I don't care how they comb their hair. Just how they play football. — *Don Coryell, San Diego Chargers coach.*

850 At that rate, he's going to last 150 years. — *H.L. Hunt, businesman, told son Lamar would lose $1 million the initial year of the American Football League.*

851 Base your play on the standards most likely to defeat the champions. — *Bernie Bierman, Minnesota football coach.*

852 Beat your opponent where he is strongest, and you demoralize him. — *Vince Lombardi, Green Bay Packers coach.*

853 The beauty of the game of football is that so often you are called upon to do something beyond your capabilities — and you do it. — *Dub Jones, former running back.*

854 Because if it didn't work out I didn't want to blow the whole day. — *Paul Hornung, Green Bay Packers running back, on the reason he got married at 11 a.m.*

855 Being cold, like being determined to win, is just a state of mind. — *Woody Hayes, Ohio State football coach.*

856 The best time to play a freshman is when he is a junior. — *Cal Stoll, Minnesota football coach.*

857 Bowl games are not fun unless you win. — *Darrell Royal, Texas football coach.*

858 California has lots of good high school boys with A averages, and I think we're going to get both of them. — *Marv Levy, California football coach.*

859 Class is, when they run you out of town, to look like you're leading the parade. — *Bill Battle, former Tennessee football coach.*

860 Coaching is like a bath — if you stay in long enough, it's not so hot. — *Biggie Munn, Michigan State athletic director.*

861 Coaching is not conducive to family life, and coaches are basically not family men. — *Jackie Biles, New York Jets coach.*

862 A coach simply must resign himself to the fact that he is no longer involved with the educational process, but with entertainment. — *Ralph (Shug) Jordan, Auburn football coach.*

863 Coach, why do I do things like that? — *John Isenbarger, Indiana punter, after failing to convert a fake punt.*

864 (College) football has to make money. It has to support the spring sports. I can show you how to have a heck of a wrestling team. Let me recruit the guys who'll get us on top in football and we'll have good everything. — *Chuck Fairbanks, Oklahoma football coach.*

865 College football today is one of the last great strongholds of genuine, old-fashioned American hypocrisy. — *Paul Gallico, writer.*

866 A college racing stable makes as much sense as college football. The jockey could carry the college colors, the students could cheer, the alumni could bet and the horse wouldn't have to pass a history test. — *Robert Hutchins, University of Chicago president.*

867 The country is full of good coaches. What it takes to win is a bunch of interested players. — *Don Coryell, San Diego Chargers coach.*

868 The days of the dictatorial coach are over. Players expect you to explain things now. They want to know why. A coach has to be a chaplain, a public-relations man, a disciplinarian, a counsellor, an educator. But I like that. I like it a lot. — *Ara Parseghian, Notre Dame football coach.*

869 Death and injuries are not the strongest argument against football; that cheating and brutality are profitable is the main evil. — *Charles Eliot, Harvard president in 1905.*

870 Deep down, I don't know how many players would admit it, but when we lost a playoff game before getting to the Super Bowl, it was never bad because when you lost, you were free. If you won, there was the Super Bowl and the extra money, but if you lost, you were free. If you won, there was the Super Bowl and the extra money, but if you lost, you were out of prison. — *Pat Toomay, Dallas Cowboys defensive lineman.*

871 Defeat is worse than death, because you have to live with defeat. — *Vince Lombardi, Green Bay Packers coach.*

872 Defense is something you play while the offensive players rest. — *Glen Dobbs, Tulsa football coach.*

873 Defense, that's where you have to start rating a team's chances for the championship. — *Tom Landry, Dallas Cowboys coach.*

874 Defensive backs. Nothing but reactions. You train 'em like seals. — *Sam Baker, Philadelphia Eagles kicker.*

875 The definition of an atheist in Alabama is a person who doesn't believe in Bear Bryant. — *Wally Butts, Georgia athletic director.*

876 The difference between good and great is just a little extra effort. — *Biggie Munn, Michigan State athletic director.*

877 Don't bother reading it, kid — everybody gets killed in the end. — *Peter Gent, Dallas Cowboys receiver, asked by a rookie about the playbook.*

878 Do you know what happens after you lose the Super Bowl? The world ends. It just stops. — *Joe Kapp, Minnesota Vikings quarterback.*

879 Earl Campbell may not be in a class by himself, but whatever class he's in, it doesn't take long to call the roll. — *Bum Phillips, Houston Oilers coach.*

880 Embarrassment is a great motivator. Some people play very, very well just so they won't get embarrassed. — *Lynn Swann, Pittsburgh Steelers receiver.*

881 Every day you waste is one you can never make up. — *George Allen, Washington Redskins coach.*

882 Everyone has some fear. A man who has no fear belongs in a mental institution. Or on special teams. — *Walt Michaels, New York Jets coach.*

883 Every student during undergraduate days should experience a losing football season. — *John Hannah, New England Patriot lineman.*

884 Every successful coach must have a successful quarterback. — *Ara Parseghian, Notre Dame football coach.*

885 Everything that has happened in college football since 1939 has confirmed the wisdom of our course. — *Robert Hutchins, former University of Chicago president on the decision to eliminate football.*

886 Every time a team wins one or two Super Bowls, people start talking about a new dynasty, but pretty soon along comes somebody a little bigger, a little tougher and a little meaner. — *Merlin Olsen, Los Angeles Rams defensive lineman.*

887 Every time I hear it before a game, it reminds me of where we are in this world, in life. I kind of thank God that we're in this country. When I hear it, I get a chill. It's a thrill for me. I can't understand why people are talking about not playing it. — *Joe Namath, New York Jets quarterback, on playing the Star Spangled Banner before a game.*

888 Every time you win, you're reborn; when you lose, you die a little. — *George Allen, Washington Redskins coach.*

889 Fatigue makes cowards of us all. — *Vince Lombardi, Green Bay Packers coach.*

890 The fear of football players is not the fear of pain, but the fear that an injury will keep them from doing their job. — *Andy Russell, Pittsburgh Steelers linebacker.*

891 Fewer than three touchdowns is not enough, and more than five is rubbing it in. — *Jock Sutherland, University of Pittsburgh coach.*

892 Financial gain is not the most important thing for an athlete. When he loses the ovation of the crowd, the athlete dies. — *Greg Cook, Cincinnati Bengals quarterback, when an injured shoulder forced his retirement.*

893 The first championship is the toughest. After that they come easier. — *Tom Landry, Dallas Cowboys coach.*

894 First year, a .500 season. Second year, a conference championship. Third year, undefeated. Fourth, a national championship. And by the fifth year, we'll be on probation, of course. — *Paul (Bear) Bryant, Alabama football coach, on his schedule for success.*

895 Football doesn't build character. It eliminates the weak ones. — *Darrell Royal, Texas football coach.*

896 Football is a game for madmen. In football, we're all mad. The perfect name for the perfect coach would be Simon Legree. — *Vince Lombardi, Green Bay Packer coach.*

897 Football is a game designed to keep coal miners off the streets. — *Jimmy Breslin, writer.*

898 Football is a lot like engineering, if you work long and hard enough you can come up with the answer to the problem. — *Charlie Shira, Mississippi State football coach.*

899 Football is a sensible game — but it is surrounded by crazy people. — *Lou Little, Columbia football coach.*

900 Football is itself the biggest dramatization of American business ever invented. — *Marshall McLuhan, writer.*

901 Football is like chess with muscles. If you line up the wrong way, it can beat you. — *Bob Thalman, Virginia Military football coach.*

902 Football is not a contact sport — it's a collision sport. Dancing is a contact sport. — *Duffy Daugherty, Michigan State football coach.*

903 Football is not and should not be a game for the strong and stupid. It should be a game for the smart, the swift, the brave and the clever. — *Knute Rockne, Notre Dame football coach.*

904 Football is not the cleanest game in the world. — *Johnny Sample, New York Jets defensive back.*

905 Football isn't life. It's a part of life. Football isn't a destination. It's a journey. — *Reggie Rucker, Cleveland Browns receiver.*

906 Football isn't necessarily won by the best players. It is won by the team with the best attitude. — *George Allen, Los Angeles Rams coach.*

907 Football is often called an emotional game. Nobody is more emotional than my wife and she's a lousy football player. — *John McKay, USC football coach.*

908 Football is one-third offense, one-third defense and one-third kicking. — *George Allen, Washington Redskins coach.*

909 Football is the only activity on any campus that brings all the alumni back to the university. — *Carmen Cozza, Yale football coach.*

910 Football is two things. It's blocking and tackling. I don't care about formations or new offenses or tricks on defense. You block and tackle better than the team you're playing, you win. — *Vince Lombardi, Green Bay Packers coach.*

911 Football has become so complicated, the student will find it a recreation to go to classes. — *T.S. Eliot, writer.*

912 Football is a game of refined violence. And it gets more violent every year — and more refined. — *Eugene Klein, San Diego Chargers president.*

913 Football is the only game you come into with a semblance of intelligence and end up a babbling moron. —*Mike Adamle, New York Jets running back.*

914 A football player is like a prostitute—your body is only worth something for so long. When it's no good anymore, nobody wants it. —*Larry Grantham, New York Jets.*

915 Football's a great life. It's much easier than working for a living. Just think—they pay you good money to eat well, stay in shape and have fun. —*Hugh McElhenny, San Francisco 49ers running back.*

916 Football teams are no different from any other groups. They are good examples of success and failure, or competence and incompetence, of inspiration and dullness. —*Vince Lombardi, Green Bay Packers coach.*

917 Fortunately, we were up for the game or else we would have been killed. —*Chuck Mills, U.S. Merchant Marine football coach, after his team lost 37-0.*

918 Forty guys who want to play football that punishes the opposition on offense and defense. Anybody that doesn't want to, let him go someplace else, squeeze grapes and throw the juice at other people. I want none of that stuff here. —*Abe Gibron, Chicago Bear coach, on what he wants in a team.*

919 For youth, as it crosses the threshold of manhood, football has become a rallying point to build courage when courage seems to die, to restore faith when there seems little cause for faith, to create hope as hope becomes forlorn. —*Douglas MacArthur, U.S. Army general.*

920 A gambler is a coach who uses a number one draft choice on an untested, inexperienced lineman or receiver from Illinois Normal. A conservative is a man who trades his number one choices for established veterans…. In my opinion, the odds are against gamblers, innovators and pace-setters in football. Call me a conservative. —*George Allen, Washington Redskins coach.*

921 Gentlemen, you are about to play football for Yale against Harvard. Never in your lives will you do anything so important. —*Tad Jones, Yale football coach.*

922 A good back makes his own holes. Anybody can run where the holes are. —*Joe Don Looney, Detroit Lion running back.*

923 A good coach needs a patient wife, a loyal dog and a great quarterback, but not necessarily in that order. —*Bud Grant, Minnesota Vikings coach.*

924   Good fellows are a dime a dozen, but an aggressive leader is priceless.
—*Earl (Red) Blaik, Army football coach.*

925   Good players don't slip. —*Jim Howell, New York Giants coach.*

926   A great passing game gets you some spectacular victories, but it never
wins championships. —*Woody Hayes, Ohio State football coach.*

927   Half a loaf is better than none. —*Lou Saban, Denver Broncos coach,
after settling for a tie.*

928   The harder I hit people, the better I like it. When you hit a guy and he
hits the ground hard and his eyeballs roll and you see it and he looks up
at you and he knows you see it, then you've conquered him. It's a great feeling. —*Tim Rossovich, Philadelphia Eagles linebacker.*

929   The harder we work, the luckier we get. —*Vince Lombardi, Green Bay
Packers coach.*

930   The harder you work, the harder it is to surrender. —*Vince Lombardi,
Green Bay Packers coach.*

931   Having a pro offense with great receivers but no first-rate quarterback is
like having a new limousine with a chimpanzee at the wheel. —*Charlie
Tate, Miami of Florida football coach.*

932   The head coach must allow his assistants to coach. When this happens,
the coach does not have to waste his time proving points to the players.
When the assistant coach does not get a chance to do his job, he becomes both
the victim and master of double talk. As a result, he has to have a scapegoat.
It usually turns out to be one of the players. —*Prentice Gautt, Missouri
assistant football coach.*

933   He can take his and beat yours, or take yours and beat his. —*Bum
Phillips, Houston Oilers coach, on Don Shula.*

934   He is not in a union. He can carry the ball as many times as we want
him to. —*John McKay, USC football coach, after O.J. Simpson carried
the ball 38 times.*

935   He's even better than I thought he was and I thought he was the
best. —*Gino Marchetti, Baltimore Colts defensive lineman, on Jim
Brown.*

936   His father gave him a six-week-old puppy when he was four, and he
traded it away for two 12-year-old cats. —*Edward Bennett Williams,
Washington Redskins president, on coach George Allen.*

937 Hold when you're at home and don't hold when you're on the road. —*John McKay, USC football coach, on how to block.*

938 I ain't been taking it in vain—it works. —*Billy Tohill, Texas Christian football coach, on taking the Lord's name in vain.*

939 I am the oratorical equivalent of a blocked punt. —*Tommy Prothro, UCLA football coach.*

940 I asked the young man if he was in the top half of his class academically. He said, "No sir, I am one of those who make the top half possible." —*Pete Elliot, Miami of Florida football coach, on a recruit.*

941 I can only speak from my own standpoint, but I think that to some degree I'm a masochist about it. I almost enjoy hitting someone and at the same time maybe hurting myself a little bit. —*Paul Martha, Pittsburgh Steelers safety.*

942 I can't imagine anyone who doesn't enjoy sex, who doesn't want sex all the time. It's the best thing ever invented. —*Joe Namath, New York Jets quarterback.*

943 I can't see anything wrong with good clean violence. —*Bob Timberlake, Michigan quarterback, on the conflict between religion and football.*

944 I can't take much credit for what I did, running with a football, because I don't know what I did. Nobody ever taught me, and I can't teach anybody. You can teach a man how to block or tackle or kick or pass. The ability to run with a ball is something you have or you haven't. If you can't explain it, how can you take credit for it? —*Red Grange, Chicago Bears running back.*

945 I can't wait until tomorrow, because I get better looking every day. —*Joe Namath, New York Jets quarterback.*

946 I'd die for dear old Rutgers. —*Frank (Pop) Burns, Rutgers running back while carried off the field with a broken leg.*

947 I didn't know what a free agent meant, until I saw my first paycheck. —*Peter Gent, former Dallas Cowboys receiver.*

948 I do not see the relationship of these highly industrialized affairs on Saturday afternoons to higher learning in America. —*Robert Hutchins, former University of Chicago president.*

949 I don't go for character building. This is done at home, not at college. —*John McKay, USC football coach.*

950 I don't hire anybody not brighter than I am. If they're not brighter than I am, I don't need them. — *Paul (Bear) Bryant, Alabama football coach.*

951 I don't know what takes more guts, to take a boy nobody else wants or not take a boy everybody else wants. — *Darrell Royal, Texas football coach, on recruiting pressure.*

952 I don't see that the officials need any protection from the press. If a play is questioned, I think it's good for the official to clear the air. If he remains silent, the suspicion could grow that he isn't certain he was right. — *Tommy Bell, referee.*

953 I don't think a coach can bring his team up. The players have to do it. The more respect a player has for his opponent, the higher he'll be. It's the coaches job to make his players respect the opponent. — *Tommy Prothro, Los Angeles Rams coach.*

954 I don't think an athlete will buy this business that they'll do something just because you have "Coach" in front of your name. Football is a product of a culture and it's got to adapt to society; society isn't going to adapt to football. — *Joe Paterno, Penn State football coach.*

955 I don't think any of our opponents are too interested in my health. — *Joe Namath, New York Jets quarterback, on his label of a pampered player.*

956 I don't think there's as much cheating in recruiting going on today as you might be led to believe. I think a lot of it is sour grapes; one school loses an athlete to another school and it immediately says, "Well, they're cheating. They bought that athlete." That's not necessarily true. — *Lou Holtz, Arkansas football coach.*

957 I don't try to fool anyone by saying we're playing our games one at a time. We're trying to win 10 games so we can get into a bowl. — *Glen Dobbs, Tulsa football coach.*

958 I don't want to say good-bye because it sounds so final. I don't want to say so long because it sounds so trite. So for want of a better word, I have pinned a sprig of mistletoe on my coat tails. And as I walk out, you'll get the message. — *Hayden Fry, SMU football coach, after being fired.*

959 I don't want to see enthusiasm out there — I want to see frenzy. — *Sam Pooley, former Grinnell football player, during a pre-game pep talk.*

960 If a coach can't make a decision outside the percentages, the school might as well hire a computer coach. — *Joe Paterno, Penn State football coach, after failing on fourth and one.*

961 If I build up another team, they're liable to believe me. — *Woody Hayes, Ohio State football coach, on why he doesn't compliment opposing teams.*

962 If I ever get so greedy that I'm not satisfied to win by one point, then I'll know there's something wrong with me. — *Ben Schwartzwalder, Syracuse football coach.*

963 If I ever see one of my backs get stopped a yard from the goal line, I'll come off the bench and kick him right in the can. — *Vince Lombardi, Green Bay Packers coach.*

964 If it's such an important game, why are they playing it again next year? — *Duane Thomas, Dallas Cowboys running back, on the Super Bowl.*

965 If it was, Army and Navy would be playing for the national championship every year. — *Bobby Bowden, Florida State football coach, on whether discipline is a team's most important trait.*

966 If it were about football, I could rally popular sentiment quick enough. — *Herbert Hoover, President of the United States, on citizen indifference to a national problem.*

967 If Knute Rockne tried to fight-talk a team today, they would laugh him out of the dressing room. — *Ben Schwartzwalder, Syracuse football coach.*

968 If lessons are learned in defeat, our team is getting a great education. — *Murray Warmath, Minnesota football coach.*

969 If medicine has made so much progress in the last 30 years, how come I felt better 30 years ago? — *Alex Karras, former Detroit Lion defensive lineman.*

970 If pro football expands one more time, I'm quitting smoking and making a comeback. — *Hugh McElhenny, former San Francisco 49ers running back.*

971 If something changes from what you're used to, you're in trouble. — *Dave Bourland, Army quarterback.*

972 If the alumni ask questions, I can stack excuses as high as their complaints. — *Bud Carson, Georgia Tech football coach.*

973 If the FBI went back far enough, I was always suspect. I never liked football. — *Father Daniel Berrigan, after his release from prison for anti-war activity.*

974 If their IQ's were five points lower, they'd be geraniums. — *Russ Francis, New England Patriots tight end, on defensive linemen.*

975 If the Russians had a football team, maybe I'd rather beat them than Missouri, but they're the only ones. — *Don Fambrough, Kansas assistant football coach.*

976 If the world was ending tomorrow, your one wish should be that we are playing Auburn today. — *Steve Sleek, Georgia linebacker.*

977 If they'll just give something for a short time, they'll have happiness for a long time. — *Weeb Ewbank, New York Jets coach, on the training camp.*

978 If we lose, it means the others have improved more than we have. — *Sid Gillman, San Diego Chargers coach.*

979 If you are criticized, then you are important. — *Doyt Perry, Bowling Green football coach.*

980 If you are prepared, then you will be confident and you will do the job. Emotion gets in the way of performance. — *Tom Landry, Dallas Cowboys coach.*

981 If you can accept defeat and open your pay envelope without feeling guilty, then you're stealing.... I can't think of a thing money will buy that a loser could enjoy. Losers just look foolish in a new car or partying it up. As far as I'm concerned, life without victories is like being in prison. — *George Allen, Los Angeles Rams coach.*

982 If you don't invest very much, then defeat doesn't hurt very much and winning isn't very exciting. — *Dick Vermeil, Philadelphia Eagles coach.*

983 If you find yourself thinking about depth, it means your first team isn't any good. — *Tommy Prothro, UCLA football coach.*

984 If you live sloppy, you will play sloppy. I can't stand it when a player whines to me or his teammates or his wife or the writers or anyone else. A whiner is almost always wrong. A winner never whines. — *Paul Brown, Cincinnati Bengals coach.*

985 If you're going to be a champion, you must be willing to pay a greater price than your opponent will ever pay. — *Bud Wilkinson, Oklahoma football coach.*

986 If your work is not fired with enthusiasm, you will be fired with enthusiasm. — *John Mazur, New England Patriots coach.*

987 If you send teams on the field with tears in their eyes, they can't see who to block. — *Bobby Dodd, Georgia Tech football coach, on why he refuses to yell at players.*

988 If you spend a lot of time on sportsmanship, you're going to spend a lot of time losing. — *Glen Dobbs, Tulsa football coach.*

989 If you want a messenger, call Western Union. — *Joe Don Looney, Detroit Lions running back, refusing a coach's instruction to enter a game.*

990 I gave Allen an unlimited budget and he exceeded it. — *Edward Bennett Williams, Washington Redskins owner, on coach George Allen.*

991 I got the best offense I've ever had in my life. I just don't have the kids to run it. — *Frank Howard, Clemson football coach.*

992 I had a friend with a lifetime contract. After two bad years the university president called him into his office and pronounced him dead. — *Bob Devaney, Nebraska football coach, on lifetime contracts.*

993 I had a license to kill for 60 minutes a week. It was like going totally insane. — *Alex Karras, former Detroit Lions defensive lineman.*

994 I had offers from the Detroit Lions and Green Bay Packers, who were pretty hard up for linemen in those days. If I had gone into pro football, the name Jerry Ford might have been a household word today. — *Gerald Ford, United States senator, six months before becoming president.*

995 I have always felt that the team with the quarterback is the team to watch. — *John McKay, USC football coach.*

996 I have a master's degree. The subject of my thesis was, "What college done for me." — *Al Conover, Rice football coach.*

997 I have an affinity for futility. — *Joe Robbie, Miami Dolphins owner.*

998 I have great confidence in sports as an industry on what I think is a sensible base. But that sensible base does not exist at present. Pro sports are in for a rude awakening. Ours isn't the last league to go. — *Chris Hemmeter, World Football League executive, on the league's demise.*

999 I have never liked the regular quarterback (to be the holder). Just the fact we are trying a field goal means that he missed a third-down play. He's not concentrating on the snap. He's wondering what went wrong on the last play and worrying that it might happen again. — *Pete Gogolak, New York Giants kicker.*

1000   I hope that I have been enriched by the disappointment. There is something noble in defeat. You cannot find victory unless you first understand defeat. — *Duane Thomas, Dallas Cowboys running back, after losing Super Bowl IV.*

1001   I just imagine that the guy on the other side of the line is a professor that's been giving me a bad time. — *Art Fleak, Oklahoma State tackle, on blocking.*

1002   I kind of screwed up my redshirt year, then had to take incompletes in summer school because I went golfing every day. — *Jim McMahon, Brigham Young quarterback, on why he failed to graduate.*

1003   I knew the Ivy League was serious about its football, but I didn't think they would stoop to germ warfare. — *Ben Schwartzwalder, Syracuse football coach, hearing of a boils epidemic which sidelined 17 Dartmouth players.*

1004   I left because of illness and fatigue. The fans were sick and tired of me. — *John Ralston, Denver Broncos coach, after being fired.*

1005   I like to surround myself with bald heads. — *George Allen, Washington Redskins coach.*

1006   I'll do anything I can get away with to protect my quarterback. This is not a gentleman's game. — *Conrad Dobler, St. Louis Cardinals lineman.*

1007   I'll know it's never been used. — *Joe Paterno, Penn State football coach, on why he wants a sportswriter's brain if he needs a transplant.*

1008   I'll live today the rest of my life. — *Scrappy Moore, Chattanooga football coach, after defeating Tennessee for the first time in 51 years.*

1009   I'll put up with your nonsense only until I find somebody good enough to take your place. — *Vince Lombardi, Green Bay Packers coach, to a malcontent player.*

1010   I'll trade a defensive tackle for a quarterback anytime. — *Tommy Prothro, San Diego Chargers coach.*

1011   I love the game as do other owners. There isn't an owner in the NFL that is in it for a buck. They're in it because they love the sport. — *Art Modell, Cleveland Browns owner.*

1012   I'm a football player, not a football worker, — *Mike Curtis, Baltimore Colts linebacker, refusing to join a players' strike.*

1013 I'm all right coach, but how are my fans taking it? — *Drake Garrett, Michigan State running back, after being knocked out on the field.*

1014 I'm expecting a good season; I don't know why. Just ignorance I guess. — *Abe Martin, Texas Christian football coach, on his prospects for the fall.*

1015 I'm old-fashioned. I hate my enemies. — *Norm Van Brocklin, Atlanta Falcons coach.*

1016 I'm on a one-year renewal, and I'm not trusting my paycheck to someone on a four-year scholarship. — *Bob Cummings, Iowa football coach, on why he calls the plays.*

1017 I'm the oratorical equivalent of a blocked punt. — *Hayden Fry, SMU football coach.*

1018 I'm tired of those NFL players who jump to the new league saying, "I did it for my family." They should come right out and truthfully admit, "I did it because I'm greedy." — *Marv Hubbard, Oakland Raiders running back.*

1019 I never graduated from Iowa, but I was only there for two terms — Truman's and Eisenhower's. — *Alex Karras, Detroit Lions defensive lineman.*

1020 I never held an honest man in my life. — *Winston Hill, New York Jets offensive lineman.*

1021 I never tell my football team anything that I don't absolutely believe myself. — *Vince Lombardi, Green Bay Packers coach.*

1022 In football, the contract is either you hurt the opponent or he hurts you. The coach must have his men feeling that they not only can kill, but that they should kill. — *Chester Price, Harvard psychiatrist.*

1023 In Sid Gillman, the milk of human kindness has turned to yogurt. — *Sonny Werblin, New York Jets general manager, on dealing with San Diego general manager Sid Gillman.*

1024 In the military, they say war is hell. To be honest about the damn thing, football is hell. — *Al Davis, Oakland Raiders general manager.*

1025 In the old days of recruiting, you could gamble on a poor student, as long as he had ability and size. Now you got to find yourself a youngster with a lot of bookshelves in his home and hope he knows what a forward pass is. — *Abe Martin, Texas Christian football coach.*

1026   In the Shreve High football stadium, I think of Pollacks nursing long
       beers in Tiltonsville, the grey faces of Negroes in the blast furnace at
Benwood, and the ruptured night watchman of Wheeling Steel dreaming of
heroes.... — *James Wright, writer.*

1027   In 26 years in the pros, I haven't noticed many changes. The players
       are faster, bigger, smarter and more disloyal to their owners. That's
about it. — *George Blanda, Oakland Raiders kicker.*

1028   I really had the crowd on a string. It was yea, boo, yea, boo. But if I
       let that bother me, I'd have to go back pressing pants with my old man.
— *Billy Kilmer, Washington Redskins quarterback.*

1029   I remember the snowplows and Jeeps pushing the snow off the field so
       we could practice. Vince would be on the blocking sled, and we'd be
swearing, "This man's insane." We could hardly stand, it was so icy. Vince
was wrapped up in a big coat telling us we were feeling sorry for ourselves.
Well, it made us realize that if the mind is willing, the body can go. — *Forrest
Gregg, Cincinnati Bengals coach, on playing for Vince Lombardi.*

1030   It disturbs me every time I realize that only 10 percent of our youth is
       under the direction of coaches on organized teams. — *Jack Curtis,
Stanford football coach.*

1031   I thought the jackhammer would get me in shape. What it did was tear
       my arms apart and teach me the value of a college education. — *Fletcher
Jenkins, Washington linebacker, on his summer job.*

1032   It is better to be devoured by lions than be eaten by dogs. — *Alex Agase,
       Northwestern football coach, on playing against high calibre com-
petition.*

1033   It is designed to prevent the other team from beating you with a bomb,
       so that they may march down the field and beat you with a field goal.
— *Tex Schramm, Dallas Cowboys executive, on the prevent defense.*

1034   It may be that your body reaches a point all at once where you are
       more prone to injury, and it seems to me that I have probably reached
that point. — *Raymond Berry, Baltimore Colts receiver, announcing his retirement.*

1035   It's a feeling of exhilaration. Boy, you really knocked hell out of that
       guy. You just feel great because you hit somebody. — *Ernie Stautner,
Pittsburgh Steelers tackle.*

1036   It's an incredible feeling. It's like your whole body is bursting with
       happiness. I guess there's only one thing in the world that compares

to it. — *Joe Namath, New York Jets quarterback, on how it feels to throw a touchdown pass.*

1037   It's an ugly feeling when you know the game is lost and you're only trying to save face. — *Ron Mix, San Diego Chargers lineman.*

1038   It's bad luck to be behind at the end of the game. — *Duffy Daughtery, Michigan State football coach.*

1039   It's like a heart attack. You can survive them, but there is always scar tissue. — *Sam Rutigliano, Cleveland Browns coach, on losing close games.*

1040   It's like walking out of a store with a bag of groceries and getting hit by a car. Sometimes you don't care what happened to the bag. — *Al Denson, Denver Broncos receiver, on catching a pass in traffic.*

1041   It's not the size of the dog in the fight, it's the size of the fight in the dog. — *Archie Griffin, Ohio State running back, on his small stature.*

1042   It's not whether you win or lose, but who gets the blame. — *Blaine Nye, Dallas Cowboys lineman.*

1043   It's only a game when you win. When you lose, it's hell. — *Hank Stram, former Kansas City Chiefs coach.*

1044   It's part of the game; like chewing gum or running for touchdowns. — *Claude Humphrey, Atlanta Falcons defensive lineman, on a season-ending injury.*

1045   It's simply gratifying to me to think that our crowd could put forth such an unselfish effort as they did out there today. — *Jess Neely, Rice football coach.*

1046   It's sort of like a beauty contest. It's very easy to pick the top one, two or three girls, but then the rest of them look the same. It's like that in scouting. — *Gil Brandt, Dallas Cowboys scout, on the player draft.*

1047   It's still the same old Oklahoma. They still have fine recruiting, fine coaching and a Miami Beach-type athletic dormitory. — *Dan Devine, Missouri football coach.*

1048   It was like a heart transplant. We tried to implant college in him but his head rejected it. — *Barry Switzer, Oklahoma football coach.*

1049   It would be better if they opened everything up. Give every team a chance to go to any bowl. — *Paul (Bear) Bryant, Alabama football coach, on bowl selections.*

1050 It would be great if you could remove your head and just send your body to training camp. — *Larry Bowie, former Minnesota Vikings lineman.*

1051 It would have been different if I had eaten that thing because we were losing or because of disrespect. I ate it because I was hungry. — *Ezra Johnson, Green Bay Packers lineman, on being fined for eating a hot dog during a game.*

1052 I usually take my wife with me on road trips because she's too ugly to kiss goodbye. — *Bum Phillips, New Orleans Saints coach.*

1053 I want a school my football team can be proud of. — *George Cross, University of Oklahoma president.*

1054 I want to thank the university for what it's done to me the past four years. — *Roger Perdrix, University of Cincinnati guard.*

1055 I will never cut a player's salary. To do so is to say that he not only had a bad season the year before, but that you expect him to have another. — *Vince Lombardi, Green Bay Packers coach.*

1056 I wish the son of a gun who invented instant replay never had. — *Pete Rozelle, NFL commissioner.*

1057 I won't feel our rivalry with Southern Cal has ripened until a USC grad calls me a sonofabitch. — *Tommy Prothro, UCLA football coach.*

1058 I wouldn't ever set out to hurt anybody deliberately unless it was, you know, important. Like a league game or something. — *Dick Butkus, Chicago Bears linebacker.*

1059 The Jets will win — I guarantee it. — *Joe Namath, New York Jets quarterback, before Super Bowl III.*

1060 Johnny knocks hell outta people, but in a Christian way. — *Sammy Baugh, Houston Oilers coach, on a deeply religious linebacker.*

1061 Johnny Rodgers is not only the greatest athlete I ever coached, he is the greatest athlete I have ever seen. The only thing he could not do real well was drive a car. — *Bob Devaney, Nebraska football coach.*

1062 Just play like you do in a game, son. Loaf a little. — *Sammy Baugh, New York Titans coach, after a player stopped a scrimmage play.*

1063 Kickers are like horse manure. They're all over the place. — *John McKay, USC football coach.*

1064 Kid, just go down and throw yourself on the fire. — *Steve Raible, Seattle Seahawks, on instructions he received on the specialty team.*

1065 Kill the weak and punish the strong. — *Anonymous.*

1066 Let's face it, most of the people in our society enjoy watching one guy knock down another one. — *John Niland, Dallas Cowboys lineman.*

1067 Lombardi treats us all the same — like dogs. — *Henry Jordan, Green Bay Packers lineman.*

1068 A lot of players really don't care that much about going to a bowl. Sure, the coaches get a lot of publicity and a pay raise, the schools make a lot of money and the alumni are delighted. But about all that the players get for missing their holiday at home is a wristwatch. — *Bobby Dodd, former Georgia Tech football coach.*

1069 Luck is what happens when preparation meets opportunity. — *Darrell Royal, Texas football coach.*

1070 Luck is what you have left over after you give 100 percent. — *Langston Coleman, Nebraska receiver.*

1071 Man o' War was a fabulous racehorse. Undoubtedly, he could have pulled a plow too, but his greater talent was running. — *Blanton Collier, Cleveland Browns coach, defending Jim Brown's blocking ability.*

1072 The man who complains about the way the ball bounces is likely the one who dropped it. — *Lou Holtz, Arkansas football coach.*

1073 The man who tried his best and failed is superior to the man who never tried. — *Bud Wilkinson, Oklahoma football coach.*

1074 Man, you're just like chewing gum on my shoe. — *Jim Brown, Cleveland Browns running back, after dragging a safety during a run.*

1075 Money is the driving factor. It's not for the love of it. You never see pro football players put on the helmets and pads in the off-season and say, "Hey, let's play a little for the love of it." You see basketball players get together and shoot some baskets in the off-season, and baseball players get together; but not football players. — *Johnny Sample, New York Jets safety, on why people play professional football.*

1076 The more I see of football, the surer I am that, when a man becomes an owner, he only has two choices, He can bow out of management and put his coach in charge. Or, he can run the club himself and make up his mind that he is going to enjoy running the club — and losing games. — *Harland Svare, Washington Redskins coach.*

1077 The more you win, the more you're afraid of losing. — *Hank Stram, Kansas City Chiefs coach.*

1078 Most of all, I owe thanks to my dog. — *Bob Pellegrim, Maryland linebacker, receiving the MVP award for the College All-Stars.*

1079 Most of the mean people are now in the stands. — *Emlen Tunnel, professional football coach.*

1080 My idea of pressure is trying to do something you're not qualified to do. — *Pepper Rodgers, Kansas football coach.*

1081 My only complaint about pro football is the constant rule changes. Every year they make the field longer. — *Rex Mirich, Denver Broncos defensive lineman.*

1082 My special trouble is that I'm now head-coaching one of the teams I'd want to play. — *Steve Sloan, Vanderbilt football coach.*

1083 My whole life and ambition could be summarized in one sentence: I just had to play football. — *Raymond Berry, former Baltimore Colts receiver.*

1084 My wife and family are very pleased. They all forgot I had a good disposition. — *Frank Broyles, former Arkansas football coach, on his retirement.*

1085 Never let hope elude you. That is life's biggest fumble. — *Robert Zuppke, Illionois football coach.*

1086 Never tell 'em how many lettermen you've got coming back. Tell 'em how many you've lost. — *Knute Rockne, Notre Dame football coach.*

1087 The new players keep getting better, and it makes you think you're getting worse. — *Alex Sandusky, Baltimore Colts lineman, on his retirement.*

1088 Nobody in football is worth a million dollars. It's ridiculous. — *Joe Paterno, Penn State football coach, refusing an offer to coach a professional team.*

1089 Nobody plays in the Pro Bowl, including those who show up. — *Fran Tarkenton, Minnesota Vikings quarterback.*

1090 No, but it is one with which we can lose with dignity. — *Eddie Freeman, Greer High School football coach, asked if a new play would help win games.*

1091   No, but you can see it from here. — *Lou Holtz, Arkansas football coach, asked if Fayetteville was the end of the world.*

1092   No one should go into coaching unless he couldn't live without it. — *Paul (Bear) Bryant, Alabama football coach.*

1093   Nothing can touch it. It stands apart from all the rest of the single outstanding awards in sports and those of us who won it are set apart as heroes beyond anything we ever dreamed possible. No other award could mean more to an athlete. — *Tom Harmon, former Heisman trophy recipient.*

1094   Nothing devastates a football team like a selfish player. It's a cancer. — *Paul Brown, Cleveland Browns coach.*

1095   Nothing succeeds like success. — *Earl (Red) Blaik, Army football coach.*

1096   Notre Dame is the only team in the country that never plays a road game. — *Beano Cook, announcer.*

1097   Now gentlemen, I know you've been waiting for my views on Vietnam. *Ed Franklin, Yale defensive back, to reporters after clinching the Ivy League championship.*

1098   The object of football is not to annihilate the other team, but to advance the ball. — *Clark Shaughnessy, Stanford football coach.*

1099   Offense sells tickets but defense wins championships. — *Anonymous.*

1100   Often an All-American is made by a long run, a weak defense and a poet in the press box. — *Robert Zuppke, Illinois football coach.*

1101   Once we got rolling, it just felt too good to stop. — *Ara Parseghian, Northwestern football coach, after a 34-7 victory.*

1102   Once we were whining losers, but now we're arrogant winners. — *Chuck Burr, Buffalo Bill publicist, after the team won its ninth straight game.*

1103   One time he bit me. Another time he tried to break my ankle. Another time he tried to crack my leg. Nothing happened. I guess maybe my leg was too green. — *MacArthur Lane, Green Bay Packers running back, on Dick Butkus.*

1104   The only president who's ever been fired at Alabama was against football. Any new president cuts his teeth on it, and he better be for it. Because if he's not, they won't win, and if they don't win, he'll get fired. — *Paul (Bear) Bryant, Alabama football coach.*

1105 The only qualifications for a lineman are to be big and dumb. To be a back, you only have to be dumb. — *Knute Rockne, Notre Dame football coach.*

1106 Only three things can happen when you put the ball in the air, and two of them are bad. — *Duffy Daugherty, Michigan State football coach.*

1107 The only time age will ever hurt a team is when all the old players quit at the same time. — *Jack Pardee, Washington Redskins linebacker.*

1108 Our biggest problem is patience. — *Grant Teaff, Baylor football coach, on the school's 48 year championship drought.*

1109 Our lack of weakness. — *Abe Martin, Texas Christian football coach, asked his team's strength.*

1110 Outlined against a blue-grey October sky, the four Horsemen rode again. In dramatic lore they are known as Famine, Pestilence, Destruction and Death.... Their real names are Stuhldreher, Miller, Crowley and Layden. — *Grantland Rice, writer, describing the 1924 Notre Dame backfield.*

1111 Pain and injuries are in the contract. — *John Niland, Dallas Cowboys lineman.*

1112 Passing is timing. It's the ability to stand in there and take a chance on a beating by Deacon Jones or Carl Eller until the right time comes to let go of the ball. Nothing is important except releasing the ball at the right instant. Therefore, accuracy means less than guts. — *John Hadl, San Diego Chargers quarterback.*

1113 People are needed, but nobody is necessary. — *Paul Brown, Cincinnati Bengals coach.*

1114 People don't seem to understand what we go through. I'm a lineman, and I have to sit and rest at least one hour as soon as I go home from practice every day until my headache goes away. There's no way I can open a book. — *Steve Tobin, Minnesota lineman.*

1115 People expect too much of the Super Bowl game. They fail to realize that it has to be a defensive battle. In our system today—the three game playoffs—you can't put together enough winning games without a great defense.... In a series of games, the strongest defensive team survives. — *Tom Landry, Dallas Cowboys coach.*

1116 People think there are great mysteries connected with the game, but there are not. It's just teaching fundamentals. — *Paul Brown, Cleveland Browns coach.*

1117 Personally, I have found that pros work as hard and are as amenable to discipline as college players. There's more closeness in college ball. The pro game is a cold cutthroat business. One of the most difficult things for me to accept is the pointed criticism leveled at the pro. Because he is playing for money, people are less sympathetic toward his failure. — *Chuck Fairbanks, New England Patriots coach, comparing college and professional football.*

1118 Players play the game, not writers. — *Johnny Sample, New York Jets safety, after winning Super Bowl III.*

1119 The players say they want to be treated like ordinary people. But they're not ordinary people. How can you compare a $100,000-a-year football player with an $8,000-a-year wage earner? — *Jim Langer, Miami Dolphins lineman, on the 1974 player strike.*

1120 Playing middle linebacker is like walking through a lion's cage in a three-piece pork-chop suit. — *Cecil Johnson, Tampa Bay Buccaneers outside linebacker, on playing middle linebacker.*

1121 Prayers work best when players are big. — *Knute Rockne, Notre Dame football coach.*

1122 Pro football is just a bunch of college players who wanted to play a little longer. That's all. It's not complicated. — *Terry Bradshaw, Pittsburgh Steelers quarterback.*

1123 Pro football is like nuclear warfare. There are no winners, only survivors. — *Frank Gifford, New York Giants running back.*

1124 A quarterback should run only from sheer terror. — *Norm Van Brocklin, Atlanta Falcon coach.*

1125 Reading your keys gets you into the area, but then it's up to you. It's seek and destroy. — *Dave Robinson, Green Bay Packers linebacker.*

1126 Regardless of whether you play well or not, you show class when you come from behind. — *Paul Dietzel, South Carolina football coach.*

1127 The running back always has a little fear in him. You know that you've got that ball and wherever the ball is, that's where the crowd is going to be. And getting tackled is a thing that hurts. You know, nobody in his right mind wants to go ramming head on into someone else. — *Mel Farr, Detroit Lions running back.*

1128 Running into the line, you go into a different world. All around you guys are scratching, clawing, beating on each other, feeling pain. There are noises from the crowd and from the linemen; but during that one moment, I never seem to hear them. Then, going back to the huddle, the sound of pads slamming together will still be in my ears, and I'll listen for the first time. The sensation gives a real insight into the game. It's too bad more people haven't been in there, where football is really played. — *Larry Csonka, Miami Dolphins running back.*

1129 The SEC gets dedicated football players; the ACC gets dedicated students. — *Frank Howard, Clemson football coach, on the difference between conferences.*

1130 Show me a good and gracious loser and I'll show you a failure. — *Knute Rockne, Notre Dame football coach.*

1131 Show me a man who loafs and I'll show you a man who despises himself and all his teammates. — *Larry Brown, Washington Redskins running back.*

1132 Show me an All-Pro offensive tackle and I'll show you a holder. — *Henry Jordan, Green Bay Packers defensive lineman.*

1133 Some of the players now — I'm not sure whether football is a vacation or an avocation with them. You know what football is to me? It's blood. — *Sid Gillman, San Diego Chargers coach.*

1134 Some of us will do our jobs well and some will not, but we will all be judged by only one thing — the result. — *Vince Lombardi, Green Bay Packers coach.*

1135 Some players are spoiled little brats who have never grown up, live in a sort of dream world. They're given special privileges, treated like royalty since the first day they ran for four touchdowns. — *Jack Lambert, Pittsburgh Steelers linebacker.*

1136 Some players just can't operate without drugs. I've seen players take drugs that would make you or me climb the walls, but somehow they give athletes the pick-up they like. Almost all team physicians disapprove of strong drugs. But the coaches want them — for some athletes won't play without them. — *Kendall Small, Oakland Raiders team physician in 1969.*

1137 Some say God never sends you more than you can handle, but God may be overestimating my ability. — *Lou Holtz, Arkansas football coach.*

1138 Sometimes the light at the end of the tunnel is an oncoming train. — *Lou Holtz, Arkansas football coach.*

1139 The Sooners don't rebuild, they reload. — *Darrell Dickey, Kansas State quarterback, on the Oklahoma Sooners.*

1140 Speed, strength and the ability to recognize pain immediately. — *Reggie Williams, Cincinnati Bengals linebacker, on his football qualities.*

1141 Sport is the only place we have left where we can start even. — *Paul (Bear) Bryant, Alabama football coach.*

1142 Statistics always remind me of the fellow who drowned in a river whose average depth was only three feet. — *Woody Hayes, Ohio State football coach.*

1143 Statistics are a salve. You rub them on your wounds after you lose and you feel a little better. — *Bill Johnson, Cincinnati Bengals assistant coach.*

1144 Statistics are like loose women. Once you get them, they let you do what you want with them. — *Walt Michaels, New York Jets coach.*

1145 The street to obscurity is paved with athletes who perform great feats before friendly crowds. Greatness in major league sports is the ability to win in a stadium filled with people who are pulling for you to lose. — *George Allen, Los Angeles Rams coach.*

1146 Success without honor is an unseasoned dish; it will satisfy your hunger, but it won't taste good. — *Joe Paterno, Penn State football coach.*

1147 Taking the shortest distance to the ball carrier and arriving in bad humor. — *Bowden Wyatt, Tennessee football coach, on pursuit.*

1148 Taylor, we've run out of time outs. Go in there and get hurt. — *George Halas, Chicago Bears coach.*

1149 TCU is like a cockroach, it isn't what they eat or take away; it's what they fall in and ruin. — *Darrell Royal, Texas football coach.*

1150 The teams that win the most make the most money. — *Vince Lombardi, Green Bay Packers coach.*

1151 A team that won't be beat, can't be beat. — *Johnny Poe, Princeton football coach.*

1152 That moment was when I fully realized I wasn't the football coach at Georgia Tech anymore. — *Bobby Dodd, former Georgia Tech football coach, after receiving a speeding ticket.*

1153 That's where Gino went to school. When he graduated, they retired his grades. — *Art Donovan, Baltimore Colts lineman, passing teammate Gino Marchetti's alma mater.*

1154 There are coaches who spend 18 hours a day coaching the perfect game and they lose because the ball is oval and they can't control the bounce. — *Bud Grant, Minnesota Vikings coach.*

1155 There are easy games in ping-pong and tennis, but there are no easy games in football. — *Pepper Rodgers, UCLA football coach, on being a 30-point favorite.*

1156 There are no new techniques. It's a job where you have it or you don't. — *O.J. Simpson, Buffalo Bills running back, on being a running back.*

1157 There aren't any tricks. It's hard work and pain and loneliness. But you can come back, that's what I want everybody to know. You can come back. — *Gale Sayers, Chicago Bears running back, on recovering from knee surgery.*

1158 There are still over 600 million Chinese who don't care if we win or lose. — *John McKay, USC football coach.*

1159 There are three types of football players. First, there are those who are winners and know they are winners. Then, there are the losers who know they are losers. Then, there are those who are not winners but don't know it. They're the ones for me. They never quit trying. They're the soul of our game. — *Paul (Bear) Bryant, Alabama football coach.*

1160 There are times when I've thought about retiring. It has crossed my mind, but only for about 10 seconds. I realize my quitting would make too many people happy. — *Woody Hayes, Ohio State football coach.*

1161 There are 22 guys locked in a feud. Sometimes they can't settle it. So they call on the hit man. He fires that one shot nobody will. He makes it, or misses and takes the blame from everybody else. — *Benny Ricardo, New Orlean Saints kicker, on field goal kickers.*

1162 There are two kinds of daring in quarterbacks; the experienced guy who does smart things and the young guy who does stupid things. — *Weeb Ewbank, New York Jets coach.*

1163 There goes Taylor again. He was great in this game. If I didn't know better, I'd say he had money bet on it. — *Paul Hornung, Green Bay Packers running back, narrating a game film after his suspension for gambling.*

1164 There is no virtue like winning and no sin worse than losing. — *Murray Warmath, Minnesota football coach.*

1165 There's definitely a camaraderie among Ivy League schools. They all play hard against one another. But they have a certain bond because

they're Ivy League. Most people think it's something to be proud of.
— *George Starke, Washington Redskins lineman.*

1166   There's no question it was a fumble. We admit that. TV showed it.
Coaches have told us if we can't see a play, don't make a phantom call. The crew didn't see the fumble, and we know that if you don't see it, you don't give it to the other team. If anyone had seen the fumble, the call could have been reversed. Our guys make mistakes, but they won't lie. — *Art McNally, NFL officials' supervisor, admitting a mistake in the Denver-Oakland playoff game.*

1167   There's nothing I can do about it, so I'm happy as hell. — *John Demarie, veteran lineman, on being taken in the expansion draft.*

1168   There's no tougher way to make easy money than pro football. — *Norm Van Brocklin, Atlanta Falcons coach.*

1169   There's pretty much the same action in football and soccer. If anything, soccer is faster. But it doesn't have the obvious physical violence that the American public likes to see. I wouldn't walk across the street to see a soccer match. — *Larry Stallings, St. Louis Cardinals linebacker.*

1170   There's something about football that no other game has. There's sort of a mystique about it. It's a game in which you can feel a clean hatred for your opponent. — *Ronald Reagan, California governor.*

1171   There's this interior lineman. He's big as a gorilla and strong as a gorilla. Now, if he was smart as a gorilla he'd be fine. — *Sam Bailey, Tampa football coach, on a recruit.*

1172   There was no way our league should have survived. It was saved by the television network's fascination with pro football. — *Joe Foss, first commissioner of the American Football League.*

1173   There was one sweet little girl who wrote to me and said that all she wanted from life was the chance to stand in line and spit on me. She even signed her name. What bothered me was the fact she expected to stand in line. — *Marv Hubbard, Oakland Raiders running back, on his fan mail.*

1174   They'll fire you for losing before they'll fire you for cheating. — *Darryl Rogers, Arizona State football coach.*

1175   The thing is that 90 percent of the colleges are abiding by the rules, doing things right. The other 10 percent, they're going to bowl games. — *Tony Mason, University of Cincinnati football coach.*

1176   The thing that drives a real pro is simply inner satisfaction. That's all.

And any real artist will know what I mean. —*Merlin Olsen, Los Angeles Rams defensive lineman.*

1177   The thing that means the most in football is winning the close games. We went down to the wire 11 times last year and won eight. This year we were in six close games and won five. The teams with the most impressive records in football aren't really all that dominant. They just win the close games. It's that kind of sport, and it's that way every year. —*Don Coryell, St. Louis Cardinals coach.*

1178   They took some x-rays, but they didn't help. My neck still hurts. —*Ira Gordon, Tampa Bay Buccaneers, after being injured.*

1179   This is one way for people to release their aggressions. I see them coming out of the stands, they are wringing with sweat, they are mad, they have played a football game and they look as beat up as the football players on the field. —*Larry Wilson, St. Louis Cardinals defensive back.*

1180   This may sound funny, but not many guys, deep down inside, want to block a punt. Oh, a lot of them will bust in there, but only a few are really willing to put their face in the kicker's foot. —*Marv Levy, Washington Redskins coach.*

1181   The three toughest jobs in the world are: President of the United States, mayor of New York and head football coach at Notre Dame. —*Beano Cook, announcer.*

1182   A tie is like kissing your sister. —*Duffy Daugherty, Michigan State football coach.*

1183   Tighten up the immigration laws. —*Norm Van Brocklin, Atlanta Falcons coach, on how to stop foreign kickers.*

1184   (Time) has made me miserable. If it weren't for time, I'd still be playing football. And I'd be a happy man if I were still playing football. Believe me, I'd be happy. Man, I'll tell you, I wish I never got old. In other jobs you get old, big deal. In football you get old, you're fired. That's what happened to me. Time got me. Damned time. —*Deacon Jones, former Los Angeles Rams defensive lineman.*

1185   To become a champion, all athletes have to be willing to give up some of the things non-athletes are doing. —*Duffy Daugherty, Michigan State football coach.*

1186   To get bruised ribs and dislocated shoulders in practice flights out of second- and third-story windows I should understand: an accomplishment of that kind might be useful in time of fire; but to what end does all the bruising of football tend? —*Max O'Rell.*

1187 To hell with the signals, give me the ball. — *Ted Coy, Yale quarterback.*

1188 To pick a national champion you should always select the team without a tremendously difficult schedule. There's a difference between fighting 10 Joe Louises and fighting one Joe Louis and nine stiffs. — *John McKay, USC football coach, on his team's high preseason ranking.*

1189 To see some of our best-educated boys spending an afternoon knocking each other down, while thousands cheer them on, hardly gives a picture of a peace-loving nation. — *Lyndon Johnson, President of the United States, on college football.*

1190 To see the boys graduate, go on to bigger and better things and have them keep in touch with me, well, I guess that's what this is all about. — *Lou Little, Columbia football coach, on why he enjoys coaching.*

1191 To win football games, you have to be able to run when everybody knows you're going to run and you have to be able to pass when everybody knows you're going to pass. Then you have to be able to do the unexpected in either situation, too. — *Lou Holtz, Arkansas football coach.*

1192 Training camp is tough, and there's some pain. But it's a good life. It's better than working. — *Doug Atkins, New Orleans Saints defensive lineman.*

1193 The trouble is, a lot of guys coming up now, they don't know the difference between hurting and being hurt. — *Floyd Little, Denver Bronco running back.*

1194 TV exposure is so important to our program and so important to this university that we will schedule ourselves to fit the medium. I'll play at midnight, if that's what TV wants. — *Paul (Bear) Bryant, Alabama football coach.*

1195 Two kinds of players aren't worth a damn. One that never does what he is told, and the other that never does anything except when he's told. — *Bum Phillips, Houston Oilers coach.*

1196 The University of Texas has only two major sports — football and spring football. — *Jones Ramsey, Texas sports information director, on his yearly duties.*

1197 Unless he grows up to be President or defendant in an important murder trial, the college football player is likely to receive far more extensive and searching newspaper publicity in his undergraduate days than at any other period of his life. — *Heywood Hale Broun, writer.*

1198 Very few people relate to what a professional football player goes through all the time in his mind. — *Al Clark, Los Angeles Rams defensive back.*

1199 Violence is one man imposing his will against another, against the will of that man. In football, we all have the same chance. I don't call that violence. I call that competition. — *Tom Graham, San Diego Chargers linebacker.*

1200 Waking up from all my operations. — *Tim Foley, former Miami Dolphins defensive back, on his favorite memory from football.*

1201 We changed our philosophy a little this year. Instead of taking the best athlete, we took the best Samoan. — *John Thompson, Seattle Seahawks general manager, on drafting Manu Tuiasosopo.*

1202 We demean the profession when we cheat. Coaching's not a job, it's a privilege. — *Lee Corso, Indiana football coach.*

1203 We'd rather have an immoral win than a moral victory. — *Woody Hayes Ohio State football coach.*

1204 We had a defensive coach at Ohio State who used to tell us, "If a man comes over the middle and catches a pass, make a snot bubble. Hit him so hard that a snot bubble comes out of his nose." — *Jack Tatum, Houston Oilers defensive back.*

1205 We hadn't been paid for some time and we were out in the field getting ready to play a game. We flipped the coin, won the toss and elected to keep the coin. — *Larry Grantham, former World Football League coach.*

1206 We had to go to their campus and kidnap the guy. He came to FSU, played last year and just two weeks ago he received a report card from Oklahoma with all C's on it. — *Bobby Bowden, Florida State football coach, on a transfer from the University of Oklahoma.*

1207 We professional athletes are very lucky. Unlike most mortals, we are given the privilege of dying twice — once when we retire and again when death takes us. — *Johnny Blood, Green Bay Packers running back.*

1208 We recruit the best players we can find and then we coach the hell out of them. — *Duffy Daugherty, Michigan State football coach.*

1209 We're looking forward to a great season at the University of California — if we can find a way to put cleats on their sandals. — *Ronald Reagan, California governor.*

1210 We spend too much time on recruiting and not enough time on working with the players we have. — *Alex Agase, Purdue football coach.*

1211 We've already got sudden death — but only for the coaches who lose. — *Al Conover, Rice football coach, on sudden death overtime in college football.*

1212 We've been in the cellar so long we've got watermarks. — *Chena Gilstrap, Arlington State football coach.*

1213 We've learned our lesson. We won't recruit anyone that intelligent again. — *Duffy Daugherty, Michigan State football coach, after a player left the team to enter medical school.*

1214 We've stopped recruiting young men who want to come here to be students first and athletes second. — *Sonny Randle, Virginia football coach.*

1215 We weren't really playing for a tie. We were playing to avoid a loss. — *George Allen, Los Angeles Rams coach, after a 24-24 tie.*

1216 We were tipping off our plays. Whenever we broke from the huddle, three backs were laughing and one was pale as a ghost. — *John Breen, Houston Oilers general manager, during a losing season.*

1217 What I resent is that people seem to have the impression that football is a tough life. It's the easiest life imaginable. You're spoiled rotten, pampered and cradled. It beats working, any day of the week. It's not work. It's little boys playing in men's bodies. — *Jerry Mayes, former Kansas City Chiefs lineman.*

1218 What the hell is this society doing to people? I did what it told me I could do. I didn't have any identity crisis. In the fifth grade, I knew what I was going to be — a professional football player. I worked hard at becoming one, just like society says you should. It said you had to be fierce. I was fierce. Be tough. I was tough. — *Dick Butkus, Chicago Bears linebacker, on being called an animal.*

1219 When all is said and done, as a rule, more is said than done. — *Lou Holtz, Arkansas football coach.*

1220 When I get to be 40, I'm going to charge people to watch me get out of bed. — *Dave Herman, New York Jets offensive lineman, on the physical demands of the game.*

1221 When it's third and 10, you can take the milk drinkers and I'll take the whiskey drinkers every time. — *Max McGee, Green Bay Packers receiver.*

1222 When I was duck hunting with Bear Bryant, he shot at one but it kept flying. "John," he said, "there flies a dead duck." That's confidence. — *John McKay, USC football coach.*

1223 When I went to school as an athlete, a snowstorm could discourage me from going to class. Now, I'd walk through two feet of it. — *Roy Jefferson, Pittsburgh Steelers receiver.*

1224 When people say to me that I can't make it in the NFL because of my size — or lack of it — I ask them to name five great quarterbacks who are 6-3 or over. They can't do it. — *Joe Theismann, Toronto Argonauts quarterback.*

1225 When the going gets tough, the tough get going. — *Paul (Bear) Bryant, Alabama football coach.*

1226 When you beat the University of Texas, I don't care what your won-loss record is, it's the biggest day of your life. We look at this game as though it were the national championship. — *Barry Switzer, Oklahoma football coach, on the annual Texas game.*

1227 When you cross the goal line, they don't ask you how you got there. — *Woody Hayes, Ohio State football coach.*

1228 When you get fancy, you're asking for trouble. — *Ben Schwartzwalder, Syracuse football coach.*

1229 When you lose, you die a little bit. — *Buddy Parker, Detroit Lions coach.*

1230 When you're an underdog you play from your heart. It involves your ability, determination and just damn meanness to go on every play. — *Woody Hayes, Ohio State football coach.*

1231 When you're as old as a lot of us are, you learn a lot of shortcuts. — *Ron McDole, Washington Redskins defensive lineman, on being 33 years old.*

1232 When you tackle him, it reduces your IQ. — *Pete Wysocki, Washington Redskins linebacker, on collisions with Earl Campbell.*

1233 When you win, say nothing. When you lose, say less. — *Paul Brown, Cleveland Browns coach.*

1234 Whoever calls the signals in a football game has the coach's life in his two bare hands. — *John McKay, Tampa Bay football coach.*

1235 The whole point to life is to maximize your emotional income.... Getting that ball and going is a tremendous physical thrill, an ego thrill, a personal power satisfaction. — *Johnny Blood, Green Bay Packers running back.*

1236 Why does a man who does not like to go out in the warm spring rain to get a newspaper, sit for three hours in a ten degree below blizzard watching a football game? — *Neil Offen, writer.*

1237 Winners never quit and quitters never win. — *Vince Lombardi, Green Bay Packers coach.*

1238 Winning is a habit. Unfortunately, so is losing. — *Vince Lombardi, Green Bay Packers coach.*

1239 Winning is not a sometime thing; it's an all-time thing. — *Vince Lombardi, Green Bay Packers coach.*

1240 Winning isn't everything, but it beats anything that comes in second. — *Paul (Bear) Bryant, Alabama football coach.*

1241 Winning isn't everything, but wanting to win is. — *Vince Lombardi, Green Bay Packers coach.*

1242 Winning isn't everything. I'll never buy that if a boy loses a football game, he's a loser in life. You'll never sell me that one in a million years.... When I was a kid and would come home after playing ball, my father would ask me, "Did you have fun?" That was it. — *Joe Paterno, Penn State football coach.*

1243 Winning isn't everything. It's the only thing. — *Red Sanders, UCLA football coach in 1955.*

1244 Winning is only half of it. Having fun winning is the other half. — *Bum Phillips, Houston Oilers coach.*

1245 Winning is what life is about. — *Chuck Fairbanks, Oklahoma football coach.*

1246 Win one for the Gipper. — *Knute Rockne, Notre Dame football coach.*

1247 Without any winners, we wouldn't have any goddamn civilization. — *Woody Hayes, Ohio State football coach.*

1248 The worst moments of my life are when I wake up in the middle of the night and can't remember whether we won or lost our last game. If I remember that we won, I get on my knees and give thanks. If, however, I remember that we lost, I am destroyed by the thought of it and regret that I ever woke up at all. — *George Allen, former Washington Redskins coach.*

1249   A yard on the ground is worth two in the air. — *Woody Hayes, Ohio State football coach.*

1250   Yeah, Will Rogers. — *Joe Don Looney, Washington Redskins running back, asked if he ever met a man he didn't like.*

1251   You can accomplish a lot if you don't worry about who gets the credit. — *Bill Arnsparger, Miami Dolphins assistant coach.*

1252   You can learn more character on the two-yard line than you can anywhere in life. — *Paul Dietzel, Army football coach.*

1253   You can't get along with sports writers. — *Vince Lombardi, Green Bay Packers coach.*

1254   You couldn't take a man off the street and break his hand and then say, "All right, get out there and play." There isn't enough money around for that. — *Maxie Baughan, Los Angeles Rams linebacker, answering critics of player salaries.*

1255   You don't beat the enemy on Sunday by murdering each other on Wednesday. — *Buddy Parker, Detroit Lions coach.*

1256   You either get better or you get worse. There is no in-between. — *Woody Hayes, Ohio State football coach.*

1257   You go to the athletic director and get them off your schedule. — *Murray Warmath, Minnesota football coach, on how to stop an unstoppable team.*

1258   You know, boys, just before he died, George Gipp called me over close to him and in phrases that were barely whispers he said, "Sometime, Rock, when the team is up against it, when things are wrong and the breaks are beating the boys, tell them to go in there and win one for the Gipper. I don't know where I'll be then, Rock, but I'll know about it and I'll be happy." Within a few minutes the great Notre Dame gentleman, George Gipp, died. Boys, I'm firmly convinced that this is the game George Gipp would want us to win for him. — *Knute Rockne, Notre Dame football coach, at halftime of a scoreless game against Army on November 10, 1928.*

1259   You must be aggressive, but you can't go completely nuts because you will make a lot of mistakes. It's a difficult balance. — *Bob Lilly, Dallas Cowboys defensive lineman.*

1260   You have thirty minutes left to play, and a lifetime to remember. — *Tad Jones, Minnesota football coach, to his Rose Bowl team at halftime.*

1261   You have to have an attitude that allows you to chuckle while a guy is pounding you in the face. Not that it's funny, but if you start worrying about that stuff, it will get to you. — *Dave Casper, Oakland Raiders tight end.*

1262   You have to prove your manhood more times in one season than most men do in a lifetime. When you don't make it, when you can't perform or you get beat or you get cut, you're cut as a man. — *Dan Goich, New York Giants.*

1263   You know what a football fan is, don't you? He's the guy who sits 40 rows up in the stands and wonders why a 17-year-old kid can't hit another 17-year-old kid with a ball from 40 yards away. Then he goes out to the parking lot and can't find his car. — *Chuck Mills, Wake Forest football coach.*

1264   You know who wins football games? Angry people. — *Darrell Royal, Texas football coach.*

1265   You pay the price, but you get what you pay for. — *Marv Fleming, Miami Dolphins tight end, on coach Don Shula's practices.*

1266   You're never a loser until you start pointing your finger at others. — *Sam Rutigliano, Cleveland Browns coach.*

1267   You take the best team and the worst team and line them up and you would find very little physical difference. You would find an emotional difference. The winning team has a dedication. It will have at its core a group of veteran players who set the standards. They will not accept defeat. — *Merlin Olsen, Los Angeles, Rams defensive lineman.*

1268   You've got to win on the road if you're going to win at all. — *George Allen, Washington Redskins coach.*

1269   You want to know what a real test of faith is? That's when you go to church and reach into your pocket and all you got is a $20 bill. — *Bobby Bowden, Florida State football coach, on faith.*

Golf

1270   Any game where a man 60 can beat a man 30 ain't no game. — *Burt Shotten.*

1271 Any golfer can use any type of swing that he can master. — *Lee Trevino, golfer, on his unorthodox swing.*

1272 Augusta National is overexposed but not overrated. There are courses around the country as good, but they don't have the same exposure. That's because the Masters is Scarborough Fair, the gathering of eagles. Everyone wants to make the trip to Mecca. — *Robert Trent Jones, golf architect, on the site of the Masters.*

1273 The average golfer doesn't play golf. He attacks it. — *Jack Burke, golfer.*

1274 A bad grip has ruined more golf games than Ladies' Day. — *Lee Trevino, golfer.*

1275 A college degree is not going to help you sink those two-footers. — *Johnny Miller, golfer, on why he dropped out of college to join the tour.*

1276 Don't hurry. Don't worry. You're only here for a short visit. So don't forget to stop and smell the roses. — *Walter Hagen, golfer.*

1277 Ever since I was a kid, I've dreamed of winning the Open — not the Masters, not the British, but the Open. — *Tom Watson, golfer, on the U.S. Open.*

1278 Every golfer has a littler monster in him. It's just that type of sport. — *Fuzzy Zoeller, golfer.*

1279 Every hole should be a difficult par and comfortable bogey. — *Robert Trent Jones, golf architect.*

1280 Every shot here is within a fraction of disaster — that's what makes it so great. — *Gary Player, golfer, on the Masters.*

1281 Every tournament has its climax, its winning moment, and if you are not watchful you will miss it and lose your best chance. — *Peter Thomson, golfer.*

1282 The fairways are so narrow the player and caddy will have to walk them Indian file. — *Gene Sarazen, golfer, on the Country Club golf course.*

1283 A fifth at night, a 68 in the morning. — *Walter Hagen, golfer.*

1284   The first one is called, "How to Get the Most Distance Out of Your Shanks," and the other is, "How to Take the Correct Stance On Your Fourth Putt." —*Lee Trevino, golfer, on his prospective books.*

1285   For most amateurs, the best wood in the bag is the pencil. —*Chi Chi Rodriguez, golfer.*

1286   Golf architects make me sick. They can't play golf, so they try to rig the courses so that nobody else can play either. —*Sam Snead, golfer.*

1287   Golf is like a love affair. If you don't take it too seriously, it's no fun; if you do take it seriously, it breaks your heart. —*Arnold Daly.*

1288   Golf is 90 percent inspiration and 10 percent perspiration. —*Johnny Miller, golfer.*

1289   Golf is not a game of good shots, it's a game of bad shots. —*Ben Hogan, golfer.*

1290   Golf is not a game of great shots. It's a game of the most accurate misses. The people who win make the smallest mistakes. —*Gene Littler, golfer.*

1291   Golf has humbled, humiliated and just about licked all the great athletes I ever knew that tried it. —*Earl (Red) Blaik, Army football coach.*

1292   Golf is a funny game. If there is any larceny in a man, golf will bring it out. —*Paul Gallico, writer.*

1293   Golf is a good walk spoiled. —*Mark Twain, writer.*

1294   Golf is the only game where the worst player gets the best of it. He obtains more out of it as regards both exercise and enjoyment, for the good player gets worried over the slightest mistake, whereas the poor player makes too many mistakes to worry over them. —*David Lloyd George.*

1295   Golf is the only sport I know of which a player pays for every mistake. A man can muff a serve in tennis, miss a strike in baseball, or throw an incomplete pass in football and still have another chance to square himself. But in golf, every swing counts against you. —*Lloyd Mangrum, golfer.*

1296   Golf is 30 percent talent and 70 percent luck. Look at Doug Sanders. He has one of the best games in golf and he's never won a major championship. Arnold Palmer has never won the PGA. Sam Snead never won the U.S. Open. When I won at Muirfield, I chipped in four times from off the green. You can't call that talent. —*Lee Trevino, golfer.*

1297   Golf on the tour is a joke altogether. How can guys feel pressure when they are putting for someone else's money? Their only concern is whether they're going to earn $34,000 or $50,000. Pressure is when you're putting for $5,000 out of your own pocket. — *Gene Mauch, California Angels manager.*

1298   He is so great, you want to prove to him that you can play, too. It is very tough. Some of the younger players, when they get paired with him, can't even draw the club back. — *Johnny Miller, golfer, on pairing with Jack Nicklaus.*

1299   He plays a game with which I am not familiar. — *Bobby Jones, golfer, describing Jack Nicklaus.*

1300   I am glad I brought this course, this monster, to its knees. — *Ben Hogan, golfer, after capturing the 1951 U.S. Open.*

1301   I don't like number 4 balls. And I don't like fives, sixes or sevens on my cards. — *George Archer, golfer.*

1302   I don't say my golf game is bad, but if I grew tomatoes, they'd come up sliced. — *Miller Barber, golfer.*

1303   I, Edward Lee Pearce, being of sound mind and sponsor, of great ambition and hopefully, of steady putter, do hereby say good-bye to my carefree childhood days and declare that from here out, I'm playing for pay. — *Eddie Pearce, golfer, announcing his professional intentions.*

1304   If a lot of people gripped a knife and fork like they do a golf club, they'd starve to death. — *Sam Snead, golfer.*

1305   If you can't hit the ball 260 to 280 yards off the tee and you ain't a helluva putter, stay home. — *Dutch Harrison, golfer, on power golf courses.*

1306   If you can't putt, you're in a hell of a lot of trouble out here. A lot of guys hit it super but can't stick it in the hole. Arnold Palmer, for instance, and Ben Hogan and Sam Snead near the end of their careers. Maybe that seems unfair, but that's the way it is. — *Ben Crenshaw, golfer.*

1307   If you have to remind yourself to concentrate during competition, you've got no chance to concentrate. — *Bobby Nichols, golfer.*

1308   If you're there by quirk or luck, you're not nervous the same way you are when you're playing well and you know you can win. Then you are really nervous. — *Tom Watson, golfer, on the pressure for a leader.*

1309 I guess he's a nice guy, but a golfer isn't an athlete. I could take up golf and do a lot better at it than any golfer could do taking up fighting, I guarantee you. I don't understand these people that vote. — *Joe Frazier, heavyweight champion, on Lee Trevino's being named Athlete of the Year.*

1310 I have no strategy; I just swing and hope for the best. — *Bob Charles, golfer.*

1311 I'm having putting troubles. But it's not the putter, it's the puttee. — *Frank Beard, golfer.*

1312 I'm hitting the woods just great, but I'm having a terrible time getting out of them. — *Harry Toscano.*

1313 I must admit the name was born of a touch of immodesty. — *Bobby Jones, golfer, on the Masters.*

1314 I never think any more than I can help. Of all the mental hazards being scared is the worst. When you get scared, you get tense. — *Sam Snead, golfer.*

1315 I never used to miss anything inside 10 feet. The last three or four years, I've been putting like other people. I've found out you can miss a putt. I didn't realize that people missed putts. — *Jack Nicklaus, golfer, on playing after 40.*

1316 In the old days, I had trouble finding people who could afford to pay me for golf lessons. Now everybody wants to take lessons from me. Five years ago, I didn't own a car. Now I got five cars. I used to live in a trailer. Now I live in a five-bedroom house. I didn't have a phone. Now I got a phone and the number's unlisted. Boy, that's progress. — *Lee Trevino, golfer, on how winning changed his life.*

1317 I think most of the rules of golf stink. They were written by guys who can't even break a hundred. — *Chi Chi Rodriguez, golfer.*

1318 It is almost impossible to remember how tragic a place the world is when one is playing golf. — *Robert Lynd.*

1319 It is nothing new or original to say that golf is played one stroke at a time. But it took me many years to realize it. — *Bobby Jones, golfer.*

1320 It's always hard to sleep when you've got a big early lead. You just lay there and smile at the ceiling all night. — *Dave Stockton, golfer.*

1321 It's hard to describe what a major championship means to a player. It might be worth a million dollars in a lifetime. — *Tom Weiskopf, golfer.*

1322 I went for the green, because that's what the crowd wanted. — *Billy Joe Patton, golfer, after hitting a water shot despite holding a lead.*

1323 The least thing upset him on the links. He missed short putts because of the uproar of the butterflies in the adjoining meadows. — *P.G. Wodehouse, writer.*

1324 Let's face it ... most of us go into the Open just plain scared. But we are there because no sports event in the world can mean as much to its winner — in prestige, in money, in just plain ego-satisfaction — as the U.S. Open. — *Tony Lema, golfer.*

1325 The major tournaments have always been the measure of greatness, and I assume they always will.... Nobody will ever remember golfers who make a lot of money but don't win the important events. — *Jack Nicklaus, golfer.*

1326 Management — that is, placing the ball in the right position for the next shot, knowing exactly where to be on the green — is eighty percent of winning golf. — *Ben Hogan, golfer.*

1327 My reaction to anything that happens on the golf course is no reaction. There are no birdies or bogeys, no eagles or double bogeys; there are only numbers. If you can get that way, you can play this game. — *Jim Colbert, golfer.*

1328 The name of the game is to get the ball in the hole and pick up the check. It's a nice feeling. — *Sam Snead, golfer.*

1329 Next to the idiotic, the dull, unimaginative mind is the best for golf. — *Sir Walter Simpson.*

1330 Nobody ever swung a golf club too slowly. — *Bobby Jones, golfer.*

1331 Nobody wins the Open. It wins you. — *Cary Middlecoff, golfer, on the U.S. Open.*

1332 Not getting an invitation to the Masters is like being out of the world for a whole week. — *Doug Ford, golfer.*

1333 No tournament is harder to win than any other. It isn't any harder to win the Masters than the Hartford Open.... You have to get the breaks to win any tournament. — *George Archer, golfer.*

1334 The old fans root for me, but the kids don't know me. To them, I'm some sort of prehistoric thing. If you don't stay before the public by winning all the time, you're a bum. — *Sam Snead, golfer.*

1335 The only shots you can be dead sure of are those you've had already. —*Alexander Revell.*

1336 Playing in the U.S. Open is like tippy-toeing through hell. —*Jerry McGee, golfer.*

1337 Playing safe and within yourself. —*Billy Casper, golfer, on his strategy.*

1338 Putting affects the nerves more than anything. I would actually get nauseated over three-footers, and there were tournaments when I couldn't keep a meal down for four days. —*Byron Nelson, golfer.*

1339 Retire to what? I'm a golfer and a fisherman. There's no place to retire to. —*Julius Boros, golfer, asked when he would retire.*

1340 Selecting a stroke is like selecting a wife. To each his own. —*Ben Hogan, golfer, on putting.*

1341 Serenity is knowing that your worst shot is still going to be pretty good. —*Johnny Miller, golfer.*

1342 Sometimes I wonder about practice. I've hit about 70,000 golf balls in the last four years and some days I still play like an amateur. —*Hubert Green, golfer.*

1343 The sport isn't like any other where a player can take out all that is eating him on an opponent. In golf, it's strictly you against your clubs. —*Bob Rosburg, golfer.*

1344 The sweetest two words are "next time." The sourest word is "if." —*Chi Chi Rodriguez, golfer.*

1345 There are no pictures of what you've done on the scorecards, only the figures. —*Bruce Crampton, golfer, after a hard fought victory.*

1346 There is absolutely no skill in winning a sudden death. It's so much luck that it's unreal. —*Gary Player, golfer, after winning a tournament in sudden death.*

1347 There is nothing humorous at the Masters. Here, small dogs do not bark and babies do not cry. —*Frank Chirkinian, Masters director.*

1348 Through years of experience, I have found that air offers less resistance than dirt. —*Jack Nicklaus, golfer, on teeing the ball high.*

1349 We are going to need a new hero. —*Bob Gorham, PGA official, on Arnold Palmer's age.*

1350   We drink too much. We live too good. I don't consider myself an athlete because I'm not in good shape. Arnie Palmer's not in good shape. — *Bob Goalby, golfer, on his fellow players.*

1351   We had no intention of confounding the best players in the world. We wanted to identify who they were. — *Frank Tatum, Jr., U.S.G.A. executive, on the 1974 U.S. Open pin placements.*

1352   We have the cleanest professional sport of all. In baseball, if a guy traps a ball, he doesn't call it on himself, he tries to fool the umpire. We police ourselves. I've seen people call two-stroke penalties on themselves when it meant a $150,000 tournament. — *Bruce Crampton, golfer.*

1353   What other people may find in poetry or art museums, I find in the flight of a good drive — the white ball sailing up into the blue sky, growing smaller and smaller, then suddenly reaching its apex, curving, falling and finally dropping to the turf to roll some more, just the way I planned it. — *Arnold Palmer, golfer.*

1354   When God wants to play through, you let him play through. — *Lee Trevino, golfer, after being struck by lightning.*

1355   When the squirrels and birds see us on the tee, they start scattering. We've set back the mating season in Texas 90 days. — *John Plumbley, Rice golf coach, on his team's driving.*

1356   When you play for fun, it's fun. But when you play golf for a living, it's a game of sorrows. You're never happy. — *Gary Player, golfer.*

1357   You can be the greatest iron player in the world or the greatest putter, but if you can't get the ball in position to use your greatness, you can't win. — *Ben Hogan, golfer, on the importance of drives.*

1358   You can't hit a good five-iron if you're thinking about a six-iron on your backswing. — *Charles Coody, golfer.*

1359   You drive for show and putt for dough. — *Al Balding, golfer.*

1360   You need 30 wins to qualify for the Hall of Fame. It's important to me. Besides, it makes a good obituary. — *JoAnne Carner, golfer, on winning her 30th professional tournament.*

1361   You start to choke when you drive through the front gate. On the first hole you just want to make contact with the ball. — *Hale Irwin, golfer, on the Masters.*

Hockey

1362 Aggressive is the hockey word for savage. — *Chris Lydon, Boston Globe writer.*

1363 All I know is that I have a job here as long as I win. — *Hector Blake, Montreal Canadien coach.*

1364 Although hockey basically is a team game, it is a game that is won by individuals. — *Bobby Rousseau, Minnesota North Stars forward.*

1365 Anyone can shop for groceries; it takes a real chef to prepare a meal. — *Sonny Werblin, New York Rangers executive, on charges he inherited the nucleus of his winning team.*

1366 Anyone who thinks that God wins or loses games has to have an awfully weak mind. — *Harold Ballard, Toronto Maple Leafs owner.*

1367 As an investment, a hockey team stinks. — *Edward DeBartolo, Pittsburgh Penguins owner.*

1368 Being with a winner doesn't make up for being on the bench. — *Ralph Backstrom, Los Angeles Kings forward, on being a former Montreal Canadien.*

1369 The best team doesn't necessarily win. That's the reason you have coaches. If you had the best team, you wouldn't need a coach. — *Fred Shero, Philadelphia Flyers coach.*

1370 Charging used to be so common that nobody noticed it. Everybody did it. There were two sets of rules, one for the season and one for the playoffs. In the playoffs, as soon as the puck was dropped, it was murder. — *Ken Reardon, Montreal Canadiens general manager, on the toughness of the old NHL games.*

1371 Did the big money effect me? I'd say a little bit. Like, I was a good hardworking hockey player one year, and then after I got a million, I rolled over and went to sleep. — *Derek Sanderson, former Boston Bruins center.*

1372 The difference between me and a hockey player is this: when summer ends, a hockey player gets itchy—I feel like killing myself. — *Gilles Gratton, St. Louis Blues goalie.*

1373 First of all, I want to thank my best friends the goalposts for getting me here tonight. — *Glenn (Chico) Resch, New York Islanders goaltender, after winning a playoff series.*

1374 For a while, it just hung there. Then, slowly, it started to peel off. By the time it hit the floor I had decided that I'd been a touchy goalkeeper long enough. I retired right then and there. — *Wilf Cude, former Montreal Canadiens goaltender, after throwing a steak at his wife during a pre-game meal.*

1375 Forecheck, backcheck, paycheck. — *Gil Perreault, Buffalo Sabres center, on the three important elements of hockey.*

1376 The game moves so fast that a fellow can whack a guy and a second later be 10 feet away. We try to call what we can see. — *Andy van Hellimond, NHL referee.*

1377 The game reminded me of my kid days when playing on a pond was nothing but fun and you didn't have to worry about a stick across the ear. That's the way hockey should be. — *Peter Mahovlich, Montreal Canadiens forward, after tying the Soviet team 3-3.*

1378 A goalie has the best job of all. The only place you can get hurt is in the face. — *Jacques Plante, Montreal Canadiens goaltender.*

1379 The goalie is 70 percent of a team's strength. A good one can make a weak team awfully tough to beat. A mediocre one will ruin his team. — *Lester Patrick, Hall of Fame goaltender.*

1380 A goaltender should have a hard skull, quick hands and skin like a rhinoceros. The skull and hands are for flying pucks. The thick skin will defy the slings and arrows of critical coaches, customers and the news media. — *Gump Worsley, Minnesota North Stars goaltender.*

1381 A good definition of a good coach is this: A good coach takes a good team and wins with it. — *Marshall Johnston, Colorado Rockies coach.*

1382 A good fighting club will beat a club that has superstars on it every time. — *Punch Imlach, Toronto Maple Leaf coach.*

1383 The guy that swings wide after we lose the puck is poison. By the time he gets back, he could be picking the puck out of his net. — *Emile Francis, New York Rangers coach, on two-way hockey players.*

1384 Helmets turn me off. If you wear one, it means you're conscious of injury, and if you are, you better get out of this game. — *Derek Sanderson, Boston Bruins center, on why he does not wear a helmet.*

1385 He who lives by the cheap shot dies by the crosscheck. — *Stan Fischler, Sporting News writer.*

1386 Hockey is sixty minutes of action with no easy way of avoiding a good clobbering. — *Emile Francis, New York Rangers coach.*

1387 Hockey must be a great game to survive the people who run it. — *Conn Smythe, Toronto Maple Leafs owner.*

1388 A hockey player must have three things planted in his head: hate, greed and jealousy. He must hate the other guy, he must be greedy for the puck and he must be jealous when he loses. Hockey players without those traits don't survive too long around here. — *Derek Sanderson, Boston Bruins center.*

1389 The hockey stick is the great equalizer. — *Ted Lindsey, former Detroit Red Wings forward.*

1390 How would you like it if you were out on your job or in your office and you made a little mistake? And suddenly a bright red light flashed behind you and then 18,000 people started screaming, "Pig. Stupid. Get the bum out of there." — *Jacques Plante, New York Rangers goalie.*

1391 I am not merely celebrating the Canadiens' triumph. I am celebrating the superb game of ice hockey and what it means to all of us. — *Jean Beliveau, Montreal Canadiens captain, being handed the 1971 Stanley Cup.*

1392 I believe that every club can cite instances where a player has been deliberately injured. — *Hartland Molson, Canadian senator.*

1393 I don't think you can have everything. When they tell me a player I like drinks too much, I say, "Good, that's one thing he won't have to learn." — *Ian McKenzie, Atlanta Flames scout, on player habits.*

1394 I'd rather find out my wife was cheating on me than to keep losing like this. At least I could tell my wife to cut it out. — *Tom McVie, Washington Capitals coach, during a losing streak.*

1395 If it's pretty skating they want, let 'em go to the Ice Capades. — *Fred Shero, Philadelphia Flyers coach, to detractors of his team's hard-hitting style.*

1396 If the day ever comes when I can swallow defeat, I'll quit. — *Hector Blake, Montreal Canadiens coach.*

1397 If violence ceases to exist, it will not be the same game. Insofar as fighting is part of the show, certainly we sell it. We do not promote it.

We tolerate it and we bring it under disciplinary control which we believe satisfies the public. — *Clarence Campbell, NHL president.*

1398 If we play better and Boston plays worse, we can make it closer. — *Scotty Bowman, St. Louis Blues coach, during a playoff series.*

1399 If you can't beat them in the alley, you can't beat them on the ice. — *Conn Smythe, Toronto Maple Leafs owner.*

1400 If you don't have guts, and you can't take it, you don't belong in hockey. — *Ted Lindsey, announcer.*

1401 If you find you can push someone around, then you push him around. — *Gordie Howe, Detroit Red Wings forward.*

1402 If you get too much confidence in yourself, you're gonna have bad success. — *Claude Ruel, Montreal Canadiens coach.*

1403 If you keep the opposition on their butts, they don't score goals. — *Fred Shero, Philadelphia Flyers coach.*

1404 If you push through the pain barrier into real agony, you get many intangibles. — *Fred Shero, Philadelphia Flyers coach.*

1405 I had fifty stitches on my face one year — that was a bad year. I had only ten stitches taken last year — that was a good year. — *Gordie Howe, Detroit Red Wings forward.*

1406 I had nightmares before every game. I'd wake up in the middle of the night in a cold sweat. I'd see my teeth floating in a pool of blood. I'd see my own eyes smashed and splattered on the wall of the room. It was hard to go back to sleep. — *George Gardner, Los Angeles Sharks goaltender, on the era when goalies did not wear masks.*

1407 I had the idea that I should beat up every player that I tangled with, and nothing ever convinced me it wasn't a good idea. — *Ted Lindsey, former Detroit Red Wings forward.*

1408 I just made up my mind I was going to lose teeth and have my face cut to pieces. It was easy. — *John Bower, Toronto Maple Leafs goaltender, on why he became a goaltender.*

1409 I like the people, the talk, even the dinners. I love everything about hockey except the games. — *Glenn Hall, St. Louis Blues goaltender.*

1410 I'll hoodoo you. This club will never finish in first place. — *Pete Muldoon, Chicago Black Hawks coach, after being fired in 1926.*

1411 Imagine yourselves sitting out there ... and a fire breaks out. Nobody can move except a handful of guys and you've got to tell them how to put out the fire. What to do. How to do it. Where to do it. Why they have to do it. You have to convince them that they can do it. And you also have to tell them that if you don't do it, it's your butt that's gonna get burned. Maybe that's where the term "firing a coach" started. — *Red Berneson, St. Louis Blues coach, on coaching in the NHL.*

1412 I'm an oil man and I don't drill dry holes twice. — *Jack Vickers, former Colorado Rockies owner, on why he sold the team.*

1413 I may have done a lot of fighting during my playing days, but I never used my stick. I think it shows you have no guts when you use it as a weapon. If you want to get somebody, you should drop your gloves. — *Dave Schultz, Atlantic Coast commissioner, on his former NHL career.*

1414 I'm convinced the head goes before the body. You end up not wanting to pay the price. It happens to every athlete eventually. In a physical contact sport, it shows up quicker. A guy gets tired of hitting or being hit. You can't hide that once it happens. — *Bobby Clarke, Philadelphia Flyers center.*

1415 I'm looking for guys you toss meat to and they'll go wild. — *Harold Ballard, Toronto Maple Leafs president.*

1416 I'm not a good fighter and I don't like to fight. But if somebody hits me on the ice, I have to hit back. It is a matter of the law of survival. To survive, you whack somebody back when he whacks you. If you don't do it immediately, he will whack you back harder. That's the way it is. Great players have been chased out of the league for not fighting. The first two years you are tested. You have to prove yourself, prove you are there to stay. You have to gain respect. — *Mike Murphy, Los Angeles Kings.*

1417 I never knew the rules. I used common sense. It's really the only way to run a game. If officials called every penalty they saw, there would be no players on the ice and no one in the rink. — *Frank Chadwick, former NHL referee.*

1418 Instead of standing pat, I should have traded. I'll never hesitate to bust up a championship team again. — *Jack Adams, Detroit Red Wings general manager, on his floundering team which had won the past two Stanley Cups.*

1419 In the big games, we try to beat the other guys up. — *Ted Green, Boston Bruins defenseman.*

1420 In the end, there is only one way to ensure a steady demand for tickets to all games — the quality of entertainment provided. This is dependent

entirely upon balanced competition — another expression meaning parity.
— *Clarence Campbell, NHL president.*

1421 In the papers, it was always Pierre Pilote did this, and Pierre Pilote
did that. And then one day I noticed it was "the veteran Pierre Pilote."
— *Pierre Pilote, Chicago Blackhawks defenseman, on a sure sign of aging.*

1422 I start hating the minute I wake up in the morning. That's the only
way to play this game. That's how you have to play it. — *John Ferguson,
Montreal Canadiens forward.*

1423 It's just not the same game today. There are so many teams that there
are only two or three good players on most of them. — *Maurice Richard,
former Montreal Canadiens forward.*

1424 It's like going out with a girl friend. You don't know when you're going
to kiss her, but you do know you will and when you do, it won't be the
last time. — *Red Berenson, St. Louis Blues defenseman, after beating the
Montreal Canadiens for the first time.*

1425 It's pretty hard to remember the names of the teams from November to
March, let alone any individual players. — *Clarence Campbell, former
NHL president.*

1426 It would be nice to win, but I've been under pressure for a long time
and I'd like to get hockey off my back for a while. — *Borje Salming,
Toronto Maple Leafs defenseman, with a playoff series against the Flyers tied
at two games each.*

1427 I used to like to fight for my teammates, but then some of them got
traded from Boston. I found out that when that happened, the guys
still on the Bruins would put down the guys who were traded. I figured these
guys aren't loyal to each other, so why should I be loyal to them? — *Derek
Sanderson, Boston Bruins center, on why he stopped fighting.*

1428 I've got nothing to say, and I'll say it only once. — *Floyd Smith, Toronto
Maple Leafs coach, after a loss.*

1429 I've said it time and again, and I know that there are many students of
human behavior who disagree with me. But, with my considerable
experience, I feel the safest and most satisfactory reaction to being fouled
is by retaliating with a punch in the nose. — *Clarence Campbell, NHL president.*

1430 I want to be miserable. That makes me happy. In other words, I think
you can't know joy if you don't know sorrow. — *Fred Shero, Philadelphia Flyers coach.*

1431 I want to take it back where it belongs, to Montreal. — *Ken Kilander, Montreal Canadiens fan, on why he stole the Stanley Cup from the Chicago Black Hawks office.*

1432 I was 14 when I lost them. It was a high school game, and I got a puck in the mouth. I blocked a shot, a backhand. The main thing was, we won that game, so I was the happiest. You hate to lose your teeth and the game, too. — *Bill Barber, Philadelphia Flyers forward, on losing his front teeth.*

1433 I wouldn't play in goal if they boarded it up. — *Keith Allen, Philadelphia Flyers coach.*

1434 The key to good offensive hockey is the same as in professional football: passing. The fastest skater in the world isn't half as fast as a good pass. You can't have a winner without a good passing attack. — *Frank Mahovlich, Montreal Canadiens forward.*

1435 Last season we couldn't win at home, and this season we can't win on the road. My failure as a coach is that I can't think of anyplace else to play. — *Harry Neale, Vancouver Canuck coach.*

1436 The mask gives you protection, saves you a few hundred stitches. But the best thing it does is hide your face from the crowd. — *Bernie Parent, Philadelphia Flyers goaltender.*

1437 The mask of the goalkeeper, hiding his expression, always reminds me of a death mask. — *Bob Stanley, artist.*

1438 Most hockey players are a different kind of people. They get involved with something very early in their lives and they have a great motivation to get ahead. They give up everything in their youth for one thing, and they miss three-quarters of their lives. We waste half of everything. We spend so much time playing hockey we can't really do anything else. — *Glen Sather, New York Rangers forward.*

1439 My face is my mask. — *Gump Worsley, Minnesota North Stars goaltender, on why he doesn't wear a mask.*

1440 My team comes first. I'd do anything for my players. I'd lie, cheat, steal for them, and they know it. That's why everyone works so well together on our team. There are things I would do for my players I wouldn't do for my own family. — *Fred Shero, Philadelphia Flyers coach.*

1441 Nobody gets hurt in fights. It's the stick guys who hurt people.... For all my penalty minutes, I haven't landed a decent punch all year. — *Bob Kelly, Philadelphia Flyers forward.*

1442 Nobody teaches an athlete how to retire. — *Gordie Howe, Houston Aeros forward.*

1443 No, but 11 other guys did. — *Gordie Howe, former hockey player, asked if he'd ever broken his nose playing hockey.*

1444 Not long ago, I put a sign in the dressing room pointing out that winning the playoffs will be worth $15,000 extra per man. We lost two straight. Nobody seemed impressed. I took the sign down and put it in my room. I'm impressed with $15,000. — *Terry Slater, Los Angeles Sharks coach, on motivation.*

1445 Nothing is permanent in this business until you have the Stanley Cup perched on the trophy shelf. — *Tommy Ivan, Detroit Red Wings coach.*

1446 The odd game is a crucial game and the even game is a must game. — *Emile Francis, New York Rangers coach, on the playoffs.*

1447 Oh, what a bonanza. — *Joe Starkey, Colorado Rockies announcer.*

1448 One team will choke. The other team will win. — *Pierre Larouche, Pittsburgh Penguins center, before the seventh game of a playoff.*

1449 One theory I go on is I don't care who he is — his face will bleed just like mine. — *Derek Sanderson, Boston Bruins center, on playing against larger players.*

1450 The only gracious way to accept an insult is to ignore it. If you can't ignore it, you try to top it. If you can't do that, you laugh at it. And if you can't laugh at it, it's probably deserved. — *Red Kelly, Toronto Maple Leafs coach.*

1451 Only 10 percent of goals are the fault of the goalkeeper. — *Glenn Hall, Chicago Black Hawks goaltender.*

1452 The people are sick and tired of mediocrity. — *Ted Lindsey, announcer, on the decrease in hockey attendance.*

1453 The people who yell and scream about hockey violence are a handful of intellectuals and newspaper men who never pay to get in to see a game. The fans, who shell out the money, have always liked good, rough hockey. — *Don Cherry, Boston Bruins coach.*

1454 Players are only on the ice a quarter or, at most, a third of the game, but the official can't say, "Teacher, take me off the ice." The officials are sharper, have better IQ, better eyesight and a greater love of the game than the players. — *Pat Shetler, former NHL referee.*

1455 Really, I wish I'd played all my life in a Canadian city. It makes you feel something about the game all the time. — *Ivan Boldirev, Vancouver Canucks center.*

1456 The six zones that matter are the four corners of the rink and the two pits in front of the goals. That's where the punishment is dealt out. It doesn't matter how big or fast or flashy a guy is. If he can't go in and stay in those zones, he should join the Ice Follies. — *Fred Shero, Philadelphia Flyers coach.*

1457 Show me a team you can talk to, and I'll show you a team you can beat. — *Fred Shero, Philadelphia Flyers coach.*

1458 Some nights, a goaltender is 80 percent of your team. In the playoffs, he is 80 percent of your team. — *Punch Imlach, Buffalo Sabres general manager.*

1459 Sometimes you do make a save without seeing the puck, but that can be the result of anticipation rather than luck. That's why there are so many old goalies in the league. They might lose a split second in reflexes, but they more than compensate by being in the right place. — *Ken Dryden, Montreal Canadiens goaltender.*

1460 Sport stops where violence begins. A sport producing an excessive rate of accidents should be modified or abolished. — *Dr. Pierre-Yves Lamarche, commenting in a report about hockey violence.*

1461 Stars from the past would be stars today. But the 16th and 17th players on today's rosters can do things that the 16th and 17th players of the past never thought of doing. — *John Ziegler, NHL president.*

1462 Success is not the result of spontaneous combustion. You must set yourself on fire. — *Fred Shero, Philadelphia Flyers coach.*

1463 Success requires no explanation. Failure presents no alibis. — *Fred Shero, Philadelphia Flyers coach.*

1464 The teams that don't have the goons get beaten on. — *Paul Henderson, Toronto Maple Leaf.*

1465 There are rough players and there are dirty players. I'm rough and dirty. — *Stan Makita, Chicago Black Hawks forward.*

1466 There are times when I hate this game. Look what it does to you. It is not in my makeup to do something like what happened out on the ice tonight. This game changes a man. — *Bobby Hull, Chicago Black Hawks forward, after he deliberately injured an opponent.*

1467   There has never been a successful team that didn't take the body. — *Don Cherry, Boston Bruins coach.*

1468   There is more violence in one football game than there is in an entire hockey season, and nobody ever talks about that. It's always hockey. — *Keith Allen, Philadelphia Flyers general manager.*

1469   There is nothing so past as a past president. — *Clarence Campbell, former NHL president.*

1470   There never has been complete parity at any time in the NHL or in any other sport that I know of. There always are clubs on the way up and other clubs on the way down because of reliance — for sentimental reasons or whatever — on older players. — *Wren Blair, Minnesota North Stars general manager.*

1471   They lost 4-0, and were bloody lucky to get nothing. — *Graham Leggat, Toronto soccer coach, after the Maple Leafs lost a game.*

1472   This game is 50 percent mental and 50 percent being mental. — *Jim McKenny, Toronto Maple Leafs.*

1473   The time for probation or leniency is past. — *Clarence Campbell, NHL president, after suspending Maurice Richard in the 1955 playoffs.*

1474   The toughest job for a coach today is handling the press after a game. — *Hector Blake, Montreal Canadiens coach.*

1475   Tough is the only way to referee. Always remember one thing: From the time the game starts until it ends, you and I are the only sane men on the ice. — *Mickey Ion, NHL referee, speaking to a young referee.*

1476   Two people fighting is not violence in hockey. It might be in tennis or bowling, but it's not in hockey. — *Gerry Cheevers, Boston Bruins coach.*

1477   The weak ones are Boston and New York. The strong ones are Toronto, Chicago, Montreal and Gordie Howe. — *Dave Keon, Toronto Maple Leafs center, on the NHL teams in 1964.*

1478   We cheat like hell. — *Father Vaughan Quinn, goalie for an all-priest team, on how the team wins most of its games.*

1479   We have only one person to blame, and that's each other. — *Barry Beck New York Rangers defenseman, after a brawl-filled playoff game.*

1480   We're all a little bit sick. — *Glenn Hall, Chicago Black Hawks goaltender, on his fellow goaltenders.*

1481 We're going to have to stamp out that sort of thing, or we'll have to print more tickets. — *Conn Smythe, Toronto Maple Leafs owner, after a brawl-filled game.*

1482 We're not defensive checkers, we're skaters. We let the other teams worry about checking us. — *Guy Lafleur, Montreal Canadiens center, on his team.*

1483 We should all be wearing them but we're just too damn vain. — *Bobby Hull, Chicago Black Hawks forward, on helmets.*

1484 We take the shortest route to the puck and arrive in ill humor. — *Bobby Clarke, Philadelphia Flyers center, on the team's hard-hitting style.*

1485 What happened has set hockey back in North America ten years. What happened to us is embarrassing, humiliating, degrading. And there isn't anybody over here now who isn't going to buy a ticket to an NHL game and think he's not seeing a second rate product. — *Harold Ballard, Toronto Maple Leafs owner, after the Russians won the 1979 Challenge Series.*

1486 What I remember most about the Rocket were his eyes. When he came flying toward you with the puck on his stick, his eyes were all lit up, flashing and gleaming like a pinball machine. It was terrifying. — *Glenn Hall, former goaltender, on Maurice Richard.*

1487 What's better, gonorrhea or syphilis? — *Don Cherry, Colorado Rockies coach, asked if he would bring up a minor league player to help his ailing team.*

1488 What you're really scared of is getting beaten in a fight. A lot of guys never get over it. I don't know how I'd react if I really got the hell kicked out of me. I hope I never have to find out. — *Dave Shultz, Philadelphia Flyers forward.*

1489 When everybody skates, everything comes easier. — *Henri Richard, Montreal Canadiens forward.*

1490 When you are the Canadiens, you cannot make excuses. — *Henri Richard, Montreal Canadiens forward.*

1491 When you are young and make a mistake, you think to yourself, it is all right, I am learning and I will not make that mistake again. But when you are old and make a mistake, you think to yourself, how many more will I be allowed to make before I am finished? — *Jacques Plante, former goaltender.*

1492 When you keep the game on a high plane, the money will take care of itself. — *Frank Selke, Montreal Canadiens general manager.*

1493   When you start to slip everybody else in the league sees it, the others catch on. Now even the fringe players on the other teams think they can score (in the Forum). — *Bob Gainey, Montreal Canadiens forward, on the declining intimidation of the Canadiens.*

1494   Winning is the name of the game. The more you win, the less you get fired. — *Bep Guidolin, Boston Bruins coach.*

1495   With the Canadiens, pride is instilled even in the ratholes of the Forum. — *Frank Mahovlich, Montreal Canadiens forward.*

1496   The worst thing that can happen to a hockey player is that he starts to think. A hockey player is not smart enough to think. — *Dickie Moore, former Montreal Canadien.*

1497   You don't have to be crazy to be a goalie, but it helps. — *Bernie Parent, Philadelphia Flyers goaltender.*

1498   You get four goals off them, or five, but the goal you've got to have to win, somehow, the great ones don't let you get it. — *Hector Blake, Montreal Canadiens coach, on great goaltenders.*

1499   You have to be born a goaltender. — *Jacques Plante, Montreal Canadiens goaltender.*

1500   You only have about five or six tough shots a night. But it drives you crazy wondering when they're going to come. From which direction? How fast? — *Bernie Parent, Philadelphia Flyers goaltender, on pressure.*

1501   You're afraid of getting hurt, but you're even more afraid of being humiliated. — *Glenn (Chico) Resch, New York Islander goaltender.*

1502   You're not really a hockey player until you've lost a few teeth. — *Bill Gadsby, Detroit Red Wings defenseman.*

1503   Youth is the answer in this game. Only the kids have the drive, the fire and the ambition. Put the kids in with a few old guys who still like to win and the combination is unbeatable. — *Conn Smythe, Toronto Maple Leafs general manager.*

Horse Racing

1504   After one of them has won the Derby, any breeding expert can sit down and show you just why he won — from his pedigree. The only trouble is, the expert can't do it before the race. — *Phil Chinn, horse breeder, on the Kentucky Derby.*

1505 All great horses are fast, but not all fast horses are great. — *Anonymous.*

1506 All horseplayers die broke. — *Damon Runyon, writer.*

1507 All horseplayers don't die broke, because some die owing money. — *Anonymous.*

1508 Basically, I've found the true horseplayer would bet on a race full of cockroaches if he could distinguish some sort of form there. — *Bill Veeck, Suffolk Downs president.*

1509 The best way to stay young is to stay busy doing what you enjoy. — *Max Hirsch, horse trainer at age 88.*

1510 Boss, that horse just ain't human. — *Anonymous groom, after Citation won a race.*

1511 Certainly not. On a horse, I'm as tall as anyone. — *Ron Turcotte, jockey, asked if his height bothered him.*

1512 Every horse I've got is wide awake and slow as hell. — *John Gaver, horse trainer, asked if he had any sleepers.*

1513 From what I understand, racing people in America didn't think it was a great year. But they could run two donkeys and it would still be for the Triple Crown. — *Steve Cauthen, jockey, on the 1981 Triple Crown.*

1514 Give me a handy guy like Sande, booting them babies home. — *Damon Runyon, writer, on jockey Earl Sande.*

1515 He didn't know he was going to run until they played "My Old Kentucky Home." — *Horatio Luro, horse trainer, on the calmness of his Kentucky Derby winner.*

1516 He was as near to a living flame as horses ever get, and horses get closer to this than anything else. — *Joe Palmer, writer, describing Man o' War.*

1517 He was the greatest. The things he would do would kill another horse. I consider Citation the champ of all champs. It was an honor to jump astride him. — *Eddie Arcaro, jockey, on the death of Citation.*

1518 A horse doesn't know whether the rider on his back wears a dress or pants away from the track. — *Diane Crump, jockey.*

1519 A horseman never commits suicide, because there's always tomorrow.
—*Nathan Perlmutter, horse owner.*

1520 Horses and jockeys mature earlier than people—which is why horses are admitted to race tracks at the age of two, and jockeys before they are old enough to shave. —*Dick Beddoes.*

1521 Horses are pretty stupid animals. As long as they have hay in one corner, water in the other and the same groom, it's all the same to them. —*Bud Delp, horse trainer.*

1522 Horses for courses. —*Anonymous.*

1523 The horse shouldn't have run. It was only 75 percent fit. But he told me he wanted to run. —*Juan Arias, owner of Canonero II, after losing the Belmont.*

1524 I'd rather be a loser at the racetrack than a winner anyplace else. —*Ron Indrisano, Boston Globe writer.*

1525 If a horse is no good, sell him for a dog. Then shoot the dog. —*Ben Jones, horse trainer.*

1526 If I had an alibi for this race, which I don't, I'd feel a lot better. —*Rex Ellsworth, owner of Swaps, after his defeat by Nashua.*

1527 I'll be around as long as the horses think I'm smarter than they are. —*James Fitzsimmons, trainer.*

1528 I suspect a majority of the population automatically assumes there's something wrong in racing. Therefore, racing ought to be more concerned about its image than any sport. Frankly, they've done a lousy job. —*Sam Steiger, U.S. Representative from Arizona.*

1529 It's a difference of opinion that makes horse races. —*Mark Twain, writer.*

1530 It's a lot tougher to get up in the mornings when you start wearing silk pajamas. —*Eddie Arcaro, jockey.*

1531 I've called over a thousand races in my career and the only one I'll be remembered for is the one I called wrong. —*Clem McCarthy, horse race announcer, on mistakenly calling Jet Pilot instead of Faultless the 1947 Preakness winner.*

1532 I wouldn't bet on a horse unless he came up to my house and told me to himself. —*Eubie Blake, musician.*

1533 Keep yourself in good company and your horse in bad company. That's the secret of the game. —*Frank Whiteley, horse trainer.*

1534 A loaded pistol can go off in anybody's hand. —*F. Ambrose Clark, horse owner, on a large number of long-shots in one race.*

1535 Next to a winner, what a bettor likes is a clean restroom. —*Bill Veeck, Suffolk Downs president.*

1536 No horse can go as fast as the money you put on it. —*Earl Wilson, writer.*

1537 No, sir. I didn't know if it would make him stop or go. —*Louis Bejou, groom, asked if he bet on a horse he admitted doping.*

1538 The people who think they can wind up ahead of the races are everybody who has ever won a bet. —*Ogden Nash, writer.*

1539 The race is not always to the swift nor the battle to the strong—but that's the way to bet. —*Damon Runyon, writer.*

1540 Racing is for the improvement of the breed. It is not for the divertissement of youth. —*Richard Nicolls, horse race sponsor in 1665.*

1541 There is no sense in whipping a tired horse, because he'll quit on you ... more horses are whipped out of the money than into it. A horse resents it when he's leveling for you. —*Eddie Arcaro, jockey.*

1542 This is Man o' War. He's the mostest hoss that ever was. —*Will Harbut, groom.*

1543 Until you go to Kentucky and with your own eyes behold a Derby, you ain't been nowhere and you ain't seen nothing. —*Irwin Cobb.*

1544 We know he is the best of this crop, but only time makes greatness. —*Eddie Arcaro, jockey, on Spectacular Bid.*

1545 What you've got to realize is that artichoke hearts can be more interesting than a horse's record. —*Alvin Weil, Roosevelt Raceway president.*

1546 When a jockey retires, he becomes just another little man. —*Eddie Arcaro, jockey.*

1547 You have to leave a little juice in the lemon for the last turn. —*Horacio Luro, horse trainer.*

1548   You have to remember that about 70 percent of the horses running don't want to win. Horses are like people. Everybody doesn't have the aggressiveness or ambition to knock himself out to become a success. — *Eddie Arcaro, jockey.*

1549   You need luck as well as good blood lines to produce a horse like Secretariat. It's a chancy thing. For instance, Secretariat has a half brother who looks like a potential winner. But he also has a half sister who couldn't outrun a fat man going downhill. — *Helen Tweedy, horse owner.*

Marathon (& Jogging)

1550   Hell, no. When I die I want to be sick. — *Abe Lemons, Texas basketball coach, asked if he jogs.*

1551   I feel like I have played in a very rough football game with no hitting above the waist. — *Alan Page, Chicago Bears defensive lineman, after finishing a marathon.*

1552   In Japan, when you respect somebody, you show it by going beyond his achievements. — *Toshihiko Seko, Boston Marathon champion, on defeating Bill Rogers.*

1553   In this mechanized programmed society of ours, marathoners want to assert their independence and affirm their individuality more than ever. Call it humanism, call it health, call it folly. Some are Lancelots, most are Don Quixotes. All are noble. Our ailing world could use more of them. — *Eric Segal, writer.*

1554   Someone once said, "For humanity to survive, it will have to invent a new religion." The religion has been invented. It is the religion of the runner. — *Bob Anderson, editor of "On the Run".*

1555   To describe the agony of a marathon to somebody who's never run it is like trying to explain color to a person who was born blind. — *Jerome Drayton, Boston Marathon champion.*

1556   Where you finish doesn't matter. The tragedy is when you have to walk in. — *George Sheehan, jogger, on the Boston Marathon.*

Miscellaneous & General

1557 All men are created equal, except for the great ones. — *Anonymous.*

1558 The American attitude toward athletics is simply a part of the general attitude toward life in this country — the belief that civilization consists chiefly in bigger and better Buicks. — *John Tunis, 1930's sports authority.*

1559 Americans seem to specialize in getting out of shape. — *Charles McCloy.*

1560 Announcers are like politicians and actors. They're always aware that they're being heard all over the world. They don't want their images screwed up by saying things that will hurt someone's feelings. Frankly, I wish there were a lot more bite in the business. There are damned few working now who are willing to be abrasive. — *Roone Arledge, ABC sports president.*

1561 Athletes are the custodians of democracy. — *Max Rafferty.*

1562 Athletics keep more kids in school than any other phase of our educational program. — *Mel Caughell, Oakland school board president.*

1563 A black person has a better chance of going to the moon than he has of becoming a superstar in the NBA or in the NFL. — *Harry Edwards, educator.*

1564 Consistent excellence, while praiseworthy, is sometimes not newsworthy. — *Joe Gergin, Newsday writer.*

1565 Everybody is out for the big buck, and television contracts are king. — *James Reston, writer, on sports.*

1566 Experts always say, "I'm putting myself on the line," as if something bad happens when they're wrong. And they are usually wrong, but they seem to maintain an irritatingly high rate of survival in spite of prognastic missteps. — *Peter Boyer, Associated Press writer, on predictions.*

1567 Fame and serenity can never be bedfellows. — *James Counsilman, Indiana swim coach.*

1568 A fan is someone who gears his life to a sport, or sports. It's a person who might seem to be nuts to the rest of us, but to himself is just shifting gears. — *Don Ruck, NHL vice-president.*

1569 The first thing I do every morning is read the sports page. I read it before I do the front page because at least on the sports page you have a 50-50 chance of being right. — *Gerald Ford, U.S. Senator.*

1570   Fitness is man's maximum development to make all of us a stronger nation. — *Dwight Eisenhower, President of the United States.*

1571   For all the sad words of tongue and pen, the saddest are these: "It might have been." — *John Greenlief Whittier, writer.*

1572   Friendships born on the field of athletic strife are the real gold of competition. Awards become corroded, friends gather no dust. — *Jesse Owens, former gold medalist.*

1573   Funny thing about finance and sports — when one operator loses $2 million, there's always another guy waiting with $2 million more. — *Gary Davidson, sports league founder.*

1574   How can you set a value on an eight-hour day of fishing? — *Norman Meyer, outdoorsman, on a $40,000 fine levied against a company for pollution.*

1575   How many millions of youngsters are we sacrificing along the way so that 10 players can entertain us in a pro basketball game? I'm concerned with how many good athletes have been scarred by injury or burned out psychologically by the time they were 15 because they were unable to meet the unsatiable needs of their parents, their coach, their fans or their own personal obsession; or are rejected and made to feel ashamed because of their limited athletic prowess. We'll tolerate almost anything in the name of winning — cruelty, insensitivity, drugs, cheating and lying.... Is it any wonder the sports field is overrun with neurotic behavior? — *Thomas Tutko, San Jose State psychologist.*

1576   I always turn to the sports section first. The sports page records people's accomplishments; the front page has nothing but man's failures — *Earl Warren, U.S. Supreme Court justice, on reader a newspaper.*

1577   I am reminded of Bill Bingham's observation of a Saturday afternoon at Harvard's Memorial Stadium — 22 boys on the field badly in need of rest, and 40,000 people in the stands badly in need of exercise. — *Robert Kennedy, U.S. attorney general, on fitness in America.*

1578   I believe that sport, all sport, is one of the few bits of glue that hold our society together, one of the few activities where young people can proceed along traditional avenues, where objectives are clear, where the desire to win is not only permissable but encouraged. — *Spiro Agnew, Vice-President of the United States.*

1579   I can almost guarantee you that if the federal government steps in, rather than spending $5.5 million and have 65 employees, within three years they will be spending something like $200 million and have 5,000 employees and it will be run with the same efficiency as the postal service and Amtrak. — *Norman Lent, U.S. Representative, during the 1978 hearings on the NCAA.*

1580   I don't know anything that builds the will to win better than competitive sports. — *Richard Nixon, future President of the United States.*

1581   If every illegal sex act were policed properly, 75 percent of the population would have been in jail. The same goes for amateur athletes. There are few world class amateurs left in any sport. — *Jack Kelly, AAU president.*

1582   If I were a newscaster, I wouldn't even be controversial. If you wrote what I say in a sports column in the newspaper, the readers wouldn't even be slightly shocked. My industry surrendered its obligation to the public years ago. They permitted private agencies to defy the precepts of good journalism. They let men go on the air, not as reporters, but as salesmen for athletic teams. Those people aren't journalists. They're frauds. — *Howard Cosell, announcer.*

1583   I hate all sports as rabidly as a person who likes sports hates common sense. — *H.L. Mencken, social critic.*

1584   I long to be free from the body that has imprisoned me for so long. — *Chris Brasher, steeplechaser.*

1585   I'm afraid that it would be bad luck for me to be superstitious. — *Roy Randle, greyhound trainer.*

1586   I predict there will be a mass exodus of sports events from home TV and radio to closed-circuit television — where the money is. As they explore the possibilities of closed-circuit TV, the professionals are facing the same choice as the compulsive eater would in choosing between a plain cupcake and a rich, gooey chocolate cake. And anyone who thinks the owners won't go where the most money is, is just kidding himself. — *Les Aspin, U.S. Representative in 1972.*

1587   I strongly believe the black culture expends too much time, energy and effort raising, praising and teasing our black children about the dubious glories of professional sport.... Your son has less than one chance in 1,000 of becoming a pro. Would you bet your son's future on something with odds of 99-to-1 against you? I wouldn't. — *Arthur Ashe, tennis player.*

1588   I talk about the philosophy of sport, the assumption that excellence in sports is a spendid thing to achieve. But those of us who cannot achieve it should not continually attack ourselves on the grounds that we are not going to run the four-minute mile; and a goal slightly above your previous accomplishment is triumph enough. I think we've taken the fun out of sport by insisting that everybody be a champion or a failure. — *Heywood Hale Broun, writer.*

1589 It is a good feeling to know that I am the only one of my kind in the history of the world. — *Eddie Feigner, barnstorming softball pitcher.*

1590 It is possible that one reason for the tremendous interest in sports these days is that so much of the other current news seems to make no sense. — *Frank Reynolds, ABC newscaster.*

1591 It is time we realize that few things are less vital to our national survival than a fall without NFL football, the outcome of a single baseball game or the location where high school athletes choose to continue their athletic training. — *Robert Byrd, U.S. senator.*

1592 It only hurt once, from beginning to end. — *James Counsilman, Indiana swim coach, after swimming the English Channel at 58.*

1593 It's a shame a country as rich as ours can't put fitness on a professional basis. — *Stan Musial, Council for Physical Fitness president.*

1594 It's not whether you win or lose, but how you play the game. — *Grant- land Rice, writer.*

1595 It would wreck my image. I can't even afford to have a fat dog. — *Jack LaLanne, 65-year-old fitness expert, on why he has no plans to die.*

1596 I've never seen a major league baseball game. I've never seen a pro- fessional football game. And that's not an affectation. I just happen never to have seen one.... I feel very deprived because of the excitement people get in my own office, for example, over who won the baseball game yesterday. And when I'm listening to the radio news, driving somewhere, and when they say who won the games, it means nothing to me and I feel deprived. Because, after all, life is substantially made up of the little spices you get in the course of a dreary existence. Sport is a tremendous spice and I feel sorry for myself, as I feel sorry for other people who don't, for instance, enjoy food. — *William F. Buckley, National Review editor.*

1597 Just walk outside and you feel it. Shine your shoes and you feel it. Sit next to a girl with long blond hair and you feel her tense up and try to move over. Talk to a couple of white girls in the cafeteria and see what happens. People are reading newspapers, and first you see the papers drop and eyes peering over. For quite a while we were so naive we thought, "Man, we're just great athletes, that's why they're staring at us." — *Tommie Smith, San Jose State sprinter, on racial pressure at college in 1968.*

1598 Most of us hate to see a poor loser — or a rich winner. — *Harold Coffin, writer.*

1599 My body is exercising and my mind is relaxing and these are the essentials of sport. — *Delano Meriwether, sprinter.*

1600 My favorite spectator sport is murder. — *Alfred Hitchcock, film director.*

1601 Never play poker with a man named Ace, never eat at a place called Mom's, never invest in anything that eats or needs painting. — *Lindsey Nelson, announcer, on the three rules of life.*

1602 The next best thing to a lie is a true story that nobody will believe. — *Joe Palmer, writer.*

1603 No matter how far you look and no matter how far you go, the greatest athletes in this world are the special athletes. — *Lyle Alzado, Denver Broncos defensive lineman, on the Special Olympics.*

1604 The oldest standing building in Rome is the Colosseum. — *Red Smith, announcer, on the role of sports in society.*

1605 One of the reasons I am looking for challenges ôutside of sports is I know of no world so small as the world of sports. The people who inhabit it live in a closet-like world, virtually unaware of anything that happens outside of our society. Their horizon becomes the outfield fence. — *Howard Cosell, announcer.*

1606 Pay your respect to the Gods and Buddhas, but never rely on them. — *Miyamoto Musashi, 17th century swordsman.*

1607 So many sports organizations have built their entire budgets around television, that if we ever withdrew the money, the whole structure would collapse. — *Roone Arledge, ABC sports director.*

1608 Sport is a right of the people. — *Fidel Castro, President of Cuba.*

1609 Sport is a shared delusion. The spectators and players get together and pretend it's terribly important. That's fine if when it's over, you say it's not. — *Heywood Hale Broun, writer.*

1610 Sports and war are born from man's same needs. — *Harry Edwards, educator.*

1611 Sports are one of the main cultural activities on the face of the earth. — *Jack Kent Cooke, Los Angeles Lakers owner.*

1612   Sports do not build character. They reveal it. — *Heywood Hale Broun, writer.*

1613   Sports is the opiate of the American masses. — *Stan Isaacs.*

1614   A [sports] journalist is someone who would if he could, but he can't so he tells those who already can how they should. — *Cliff Temple, British writer.*

1615   Sports tell anyone who watches intelligently about the times in which we live—about managed news and corporate politics, about race and terror and what the process of aging does to a strong man. If that sounds grim, there is courage and high humor, too. — *Roger Kahn, writer.*

1616   Success is a journey, not a destination. — *Anonymous.*

1617   Success is no longer a matter of doubt but only a matter of time. — *John Rote, field hockey player.*

1618   That which doesn't kill me only makes me stronger. — *Jeremiah Morris.*

1619   There are two professions that one can be hired at with little experience. One is prostitution. The other is sportscasting. Too frequently, they become the same. — *Howard Cosell, announcer.*

1620   There is no substitute for athletics. — *Robert Kennedy, U.S. attorney general.*

1621   There is no substitute for victory. — *General Douglas MacArthur.*

1622   There's nothing equal to winning a big score. Not sex. Nothing. It's as close to royalty as a bourgeoise will get. — *Gary Dascoli, dog race bettor.*

1623   There's sort of a universal wish among all of us to be the great American sports hero. Thurber once said that 95 percent of the male population puts themselves to sleep striking out the lineup of the New York Yankees. It's the great daydream, an idea that you never quite give up. Always, somewhere in the back of your mind, you believe that Casey Stengel will give you a call. — *George Plimpton, writer.*

1624   The time given athletic contests and injuries incurred on the playing field are part of the price which the English-speaking race has paid for being world conquerors. — *Henry Cabot Lodge, statesman.*

1625   To be able to fill leisure intelligently is the last product of civilization. — *Bertrand Russell.*

1626 Too many people in this world confuse the ability of doing with the quality of being. — *Willard Mullin, sports cartoonist.*

1627 To put it bluntly, the players in my era in both football and baseball couldn't even shine the shoes of the great stars we have today. We have football players who are great track stars and can run at near-record speed wearing full equipment. The kids are bigger and stronger and they are all specialists. The pitchers in baseball throw harder and more scientifically, with better control. The batters go for the long ball and they can hit it out of sight. — *Wes Fesler, former Ohio State football coach.*

1628 Victory is a worthy result for which to strive fairly. — *Paul Helms.*

1629 We do not have cross-country and we do not have pole vaulting. — *Gerald Curtin, Sing-Sing Prison recreation director, on the annual field day.*

1630 We figure anything less than death is a minor accident. — *Bill Muncey, hydroplane racer, on the dangers of the sport.*

1631 We have progressed by disaster. — *Clarence Houston, NCAA president in 1958.*

1632 Well-meaning people often ask sports writers, even middle-aged sports writers, what they are going to do when they grow up. — *Robert Lipsyte, New York Times writer.*

1633 Whenever I feel the urge to exercise, I lie down until it passes over. — *Robert Hutchins, University of Chicago president.*

1634 When I ski, I ski. I am all alone with the mountain. I leave everything else behind. — *Jean-Claude Killy, skier.*

1635 When you are discussing a successful coach, you are not necessarily drawing the profile of an entirely healthy person. — *Bruce Ogilvie, sports psychologist.*

1636 The will to win is worthless if you do not have the will to prepare. — *Thane Yost, writer.*

1637 Without heroes, we are all plain people and don't know how far we can go. — *Bernard Malamud, author of "The Natural."*

1638 Working men sweat and sweating men stink, and my wife doesn't like stinking men. — *Thomas (Amarillo Slim) Pearson, gambler, on why gambling is his profession.*

1639 The world of sport has everything the world of politics lacks and longs for. They have more pageantry and even more dignity than most occasions in American life, more teamwork, more unity and more certainty at the end than most things. — *James Reston, author of "Sports and Politics in America."*

Mountain Climbing

1640 Nobody does it for scientific reasons. Science is used to raise money for the expeditions, but you really climb for the hell of it. — *Edmund Hillary, mountain climber, on why he climbs.*

1641 The reason we succeeded where other attempts failed is that we are able to stand sheer tedium. — *Dean Caldwell, mountain climber, after being the first person to climb El Capitan.*

1642 Thousands of tired, nerve-shaken, over-civilized people are beginning to find out that going to the mountains is going home. — *John Muir, mountain climber.*

1643 The view from the top is not worth the climb. — *Bernard Segger, mountain climber, after climbing Mount McKinley.*

1644 We've knocked the bastard off. — *Edmund Hillary, mountain climber, after climbing Mount Everest.*

1645 When you're worn out, death looks better than life. — *Pierre Mazeaud, mountain climber.*

Olympics

1646 Although the United States would prefer not to withdraw from the Olympic Games scheduled in Moscow this summer, the Soviet Union must realize that its continued aggressive actions will endanger both the participation of athletes and the travel to Moscow by spectators who would normally wish to attend the Olympic Games. — *Jimmy Carter, President of the United States, withdrawing the U.S. from the 1980 Olympics.*

1647 The biggest problem today is that the Olympic Games have become so important that political people want to take control of them. Our only salvation is to keep free from politics. — *Avery Brundage, Olympic president, at the 1964 Olympics.*

1648 The greater and more important the Olympic Games become, the more they are open to commercial, political, and now, criminal pressure. — *Avery Brundage, Olympic president, after 11 Israeli athletes were murdered during the 1972 Olympics.*

1649 I am not interested in medals or titles. I don't need them. I need the love of the public and I fight for it. — *Olga Korbut, Russian gymnast.*

1650 I had a teacher once who told me that I'd have to learn that there was more to life than hockey. Looking back, I figure, what did she know? — *Mike Eruzione, U.S. hockey captain.*

1651 I have often thought of those many Olympic winners who have, unknown to the world, died from disease. — *Paavo Nurmi, Finnish middle distance gold medalist.*

1652 I hope East Germany wins all the medals. It would shake our people up. I hate inefficiency. Our country is not getting the most out of its potential. — *Mac Wilkins, U.S. discus gold medalist.*

1653 I know how to smile, I know how to laugh, I know how to play. But I know how to do these things only after I have finished my mission. — *Nadia Comaneci, Rumanian gymnist.*

1654 If nobody plays, everybody is equal. — *Harry Edwards, educator, calling for a black boycott of the 1968 Olympics.*

1655 If participation in sport is to be stopped every time laws of humanity are violated, there will never be any international contests. — *Avery Brundage, Olympic president.*

1656 I have seen many things in life, many things in war and I have cried many times in my life. But when the runner carries the flame into the stadium, and the birds are freed and all the flags in the world are flying, I cry. I must cry. — *Jules Ladoumegue, French middle distance silver medalist, on the opening ceremony.*

1657 It felt like a regular jump. — *Bob Beamon, U.S. long jump gold medalist, after breaking the world record by nearly two feet.*

1658 I wasn't invited to shake hands with Hitler, but I wasn't invited to the White House to shake hands with the President either. — *Jesse Owens, U.S. four-time gold medalist, on prejudice in the U.S.*

1659   A lifetime of training for just ten seconds. — *Jesse Owens, U.S. four-time gold medalist, minutes before the 100 meter final.*

1660   The marathon is a very boring race. — *Emil Zatopek, Czechoslovakian marathon gold medalist, after winning his first attempt at the race.*

1661   The most important thing in the Olympic Games is not winning, but taking part; the essential thing in life is not conquering, but fighting well. — *Pierre de Coubertin, founder of the modern Olympic Games.*

1662   Nothing is more synonymous of our national success than is our national success in athletics. — *Douglas MacArthur, U.S. Olympic Committee president.*

1663   The Olympics are more for the average players. Going to the Olympics is their last chance at glory. — *Elvin Hayes, Houston Rockets center, on why he did not play in the Olympics.*

1664   The Olympics could be beautiful if they just let the athletes get together and run it together, instead of having us all stand up on some podium so the world can count how many medals each country won. — *John Carlos, U.S. sprint bronze medalist.*

1665   The Olympics should be a contest of all sportsmen, with no regard for color, race or wealth. — *Karl Schranz, Austrian skier, after being disqualified for professionalism.*

1666   People who say the Games are (too) nationalistic are ones who never had the opportunity of standing atop the victory stand. It's a tremendous feeling when you stand there and watch your flag fly above all the others. For me it was the fulfillment of a nine year dream. And I couldn't forget the country that brought me there. — *Jesse Owens, former Olympic champion.*

1667   Propaganda for politicians and gratification of human vanity. — *Thomas Keller, International Sports Federation chairman, on the Olympics.*

1668   The rest of us are children. — *Igor Ter-Ovanesyan, Russian long jumper, after hearing of Bob Beamon's shattering world record.*

1669   Some guys go to war for their country, and these guys won't even play basketball for it. — *Kevin Loughery, New York Nets coach, on the players who refuse to play in the Olympics.*

1670   Sports is an international phenomenon, like science or music. — *Avery Brundage, Olympic president.*

1671 Start shaving, I guess. — *Bob Mathias, 17-year-old decathlon gold medalist, asked how he would celebrate his decathlon victory.*

1672 Thanks, King. — *Jim Thorpe, U.S. decathlon gold medalist, after Sweden's King Gustav V told him he was the world's greatest athlete.*

1673 This flag dips to no earthly king. — *Ralph Rose, U.S. flag-bearer in 1908.*

1674 Under the Soviet system, everyone is subservient to the state. The Russians are no more professional than the Americans, who give their athletes free college educations. — *Avery Brundage, Olympic president, asked about Soviet professionalism.*

1675 The United States, and every country of power in the world, should do everything possible to keep — indeed, to improve — the Olympic program. Only an Olympian can fully realize the grip the Games have on the youth of the world, and this is especially true throughout the U.S. The Olympic image has far more influence than a great majority realize, and I still have the mail to prove it. Problems can be solved — must be solved. If we lose the Olympics and all they represent, our civilization will have taken a sad step backward. — *Jesse Owens, former Olympic champion.*

1676 We should send the NBA champs to represent us in basketball at the Olympics. And, if the Russians don't like it, then tell them to go to hell. — *Bobby Knight, Indiana basketball coach, on the 1976 Olympics.*

1677 A world record is made to be broken, but an Olympic title is forever. — *Gaston Reiff, Belgian middle-distance gold medalist.*

1678 Yes, we are victorious. — *Spiridon Louis, Greek marathon gold medalist, after winning the race in the first modern Olympics in 1896.*

1679 You don't see anyone defecting from America, do you? There must be something right with the system. — *John Powell, U.S. discus thrower.*

1680 You can't be common because the common man goes nowhere. You have got to be uncommon. — *Herb Brooks, U.S. hockey coach.*

1681 You're playing worse every day, and right now you're playing like the middle of next month. — *Herb Brooks, U.S. hockey coach, to the U.S. team.*

Pool (& Billiards)

1682 Bums play pool, gentlemen play billiards. — *Danny McGoorty, billiard player.*

1683 Every player's an egotist. You get four drinks in a guy and he's never lost a game; you get 10 in him and he's never missed a shot. — *Don Willis, pool player.*

1684 Fats, you ever get the feeling you just can't miss? Well, I've got that feeling. — *Paul Newman, as Fast Eddie in "The Hustler," to Minnesota Fats.*

1685 Greater love hath no man than to lay down his life behind the eight ball. — *Luther Lassiter, pool player.*

1686 A hustler is anyone who has to make a living. — *New York Fats, pool player.*

1686a Proficiency at billiards reflects a misspent life. — *Anonymous.*

1687 Show me a man who doesn't cheat and I'll show you a man I can beat. — *Will Johnston, pool player.*

1688 Women really shoot billiards as well as men; we just miss more often. — *Dorothy Wise, pool player.*

Rodeo

1689 If I'm reincarnated, I want to come back as a bucking horse. You work eight seconds, then eat and sleep the rest of the time. — *Pete Gay, rodeo cowboy.*

1690 The rodeo cowboy represents the last frontier of the pure, unpampered athlete. — *Gordon Hanson, Rodeo Cowboys Association spokesman.*

Soccer

1691 Enthusiasm is everything. It must be as taut and vibrating as a guitar string. — *Pele, soccer player.*

1692   Fifty years from now, soccer will supplant football as it is now played in the colleges. — *Branch Rickey, baseball owner in 1940.*

1693   Five. That's how long it takes for naturalization, isn't it? — *Rinus Michels, Los Angeles Aztecs coach, on the number of years needed to produce an American soccer star.*

1694   Soccer is such a simple game. It's made difficult by coaches. — *Alan Hinton, Seattle Sounders coach.*

1695   The tension is so bad. You know if you make a mistake, it ain't just your club you're hurting; you're hurting the whole nation. — *Nobby Stiles, English soccer player, on the World Cup tournament.*

1696   The way some people talk about [soccer], you'd think the result of one game was a matter of life and death. They don't understand. It's more than that. — *Bill Shankly, Liverpool soccer manager.*

1697   Win or die. — *Mobutu SeSe Seko, President of Zaïre, to his 1974 World Cup soccer team.*

1698   You can have all the bloody superstars in the world, but if you don't have a few unselfish players willing to run their tails off, you're going to get beat. — *Eddie Firmani, New York Cosmos coach.*

Tennis

1699   Americans get patriotic when they're outside of America. When you're in America, it's a totally different picture. — *Rosie Casals, tennis player.*

1700   Any human life is as unimportant to the scheme of things as any single grain of sand is to the Sahara. At least that's what I believe. I don't know what you want to do with your life, but I intend to enjoy mine. — *Gardnar Mulloy, tennis player, on why tennis is his profession.*

1701   The better you become, the more people will try to find something wrong with you. — *Robert Lansdorp, tennis coach.*

1702   Concerning the limits and limitations of the women's game — why should we believe there are any? — *Helen Wills Moody, former tennis player.*

1703   Every time you win, it diminishes the fear a little bit. You never really cancel the fear of losing; you keep challenging it. — *Arthur Ashe, tennis player.*

1704   From tennis you learn responsibility. A direct confrontation with the guy across the net, one against one, in full view of the public, builds as much character as getting along with others. — *Bill Talbert, tennis player.*

1705   Four out of five points are won on your opponent's errors. So just hit the ball back over the net. — *Bill Talbert, tennis player.*

1706   Give me Willie Mays, aged 10, and I'll make him the greatest tennis player in the world. — *Bill Talbert, tennis coach, on the absence of blacks from tennis.*

1707   He can drive you nuts at times with all that nonsense of his. You get the urge to kill him.... But he's worth the price of admission. That's to his credit. — *Clark Graebner, tennis player, on Ilie Nastase.*

1708   He has one weakness. He can never say his opponent played well. That's why it feels good to beat him and that's why other players would rather beat him than any other player. — *Bjorn Borg, tennis player, on Jimmy Connors.*

1709   I can feel my serve from my toes to my fingertips. I don't have to look, it just flows. — *Arthur Ashe, tennis player.*

1710   I can hit any shot in the book that (Rod) Laver can. — *Billie Jean King, tennis player, on women's tennis.*

1711   I don't think I've ever held a racket in my hand.... There's got to be somebody in the U.S. who isn't trying to play tennis and stinking up the court. — *Isaac Asimov, writer.*

1712   If I smile and laugh out there, I'll lose concentration. — *Chris Evert, tennis player, on why she hides her emotions on the court.*

1713   If I think a call is wrong, I'll ask about it. I figure that's my right. — *John McEnroe, tennis player, on line calls.*

1714   If I were Borg, I wouldn't talk to you guys either. He's the best thing that ever happened to Sweden, and you treat him like shit. — *John McEnroe, tennis player, to the Swedish press regarding Bjorn Borg.*

1715   If someone says it's not feminine, I say screw it. — *Rosie Casals, tennis player, on whether playing tennis is unfeminine.*

1716 If tennis tournaments could be divided into sexes, the Italian Championships would be flamboyantly feminine. They look lovely. They would have an irresistable charm. They are infuriating. There are times when the botchery is carried so far it is almost an art form. — *Rex Bellemy, author of "The Tennis Set", on the Italian Open.*

1717 If you have confidence, you have patience. Confidence, that is everything. — *Ilie Nastase, tennis player.*

1718 If you play professionally, you train to play as well as you can and you accept what happens. I'm no longer afraid of losing, I spend more time preparing and less regretting. — *Virginia Wade, tennis player.*

1719 If you see a tennis player who looks as if he is working very hard, then that means he isn't very good. — *Helen Wills Moody, former tennis player.*

1720 I hate losing more than I love winning. — *Jimmy Connors, tennis player.*

1721 I have a friend who is a nun, and her social life is better than mine. — *Wendy Turnbull, tennis player, on her social life during the playing season.*

1722 I hope it's the record. That'd be some sort of compensation. — *Lenny Schloss, tennis player, after losing a 48-46, 49-47 match.*

1723 I'll tell you how much I care. I have a dream that comes all the time during Wimbledon. Finally, I win this s.o.b. tournament, and I take my trophy and go all around the stadium, bowing to the people and giving the finger to everybody. Then I take my rackets and break them up in my hands. I throw them in the river, and I stop playing tennis. — *Ilie Nastase, tennis player and two-time Wimbledon final loser, asked if he still cared about winning Wimbledon.*

1724 I'm not really a believer in the well-rounded individual; it often means that a person has no particular distinction. — *Billie Jean King, tennis player, supporting young players who turn professional.*

1725 In Czechoslovakia, there is no such thing as freedom of the press. In the United States, there is no such thing as freedom from the press. — *Martina Navratilova, tennis player.*

1726 In school, the tennis is spoon-fed. Out on the circuit, it's murder. The coach has you dressed, fed, watered and off you go. You get out there on the circuit and, man, nobody gives a damn if you live or die. — *Bill Wright, California–Berkeley tennis coach.*

1727 I say let the kid eat dust out there. Let him suffer. If he doesn't, he won't be a champion. Buy the cheapest racket you can find and go from there.
— *Gardnar Mulloy, tennis player, on teaching children the game.*

1728 It is not how you hold your racket, it's how you hold your mind.
— *Perry Jones, U.S. Davis Cup captain.*

1729 It's always the same. Either it's rainy with sunny intervals or sunny with rainy intervals. — *Pat DuPre, tennis player, on Wimbledon weather reports.*

1730 It's much easier to play against someone you really hate. My problem is there aren't too many people I don't like. — *Martina Navratilova, tennis player.*

1731 It's the pinnacle, the zenith. That's it — you're on top of the mountain. Forty years from now I can tell my grandchildren, "In 1975, I was the best tennis player in the whole world." It doesn't matter how long you're there, or if you ever get there again, you got there. Not too many ever get there in anything. It's a damn exclusive club. — *Arthur Ashe, tennis player, on being rated number one.*

1732 It's tough being on top. It's lonely there. It's lonely because the other players are so competitive. If you want to be the best, you can't be best friends with everybody. — *Chris Evert, tennis player.*

1733 I've been around enough number one players to know that I never want to be ranked number one.... I've known since I was 19 that I didn't like the lifestyle you have to live to get to be number one. — *Kristien Shaw, tennis player.*

1734 Just because you happen to get angry at a call doesn't mean you're a bad guy. — *John McEnroe, tennis player.*

1735 Mixed doubles are always starting divorces. If you play with your wife, you fight with her; if you play with somebody else, she fights with you.
— *Sidney Wood.*

1736 Money is everything in sports. It has made me a star.... The guy in the factory can relate to me. He says, "If she makes all that much, she must be good." — *Billie Jean King, tennis player, on the effects of larger women's prize funds.*

1737 People don't seem to understand that it's a damn war out there. Maybe my methods aren't socially acceptable to some, but it's what I have to do to survive. I don't go out there to love my enemy, I go out there to squash him. — *Jimmy Connors, tennis player.*

1738 Players in every sport are spoiled today, but tennis is the worst. — *Henri Richard, former Montreal Canadien.*

1739 The prayers I have now are not necessarily to win every match, but to have the right attitude on court, to know I fought the good fight. — *Stan Smith, tennis player, on aging.*

1740 Some people get so all they want out of life is food, sex, clothes and a well-strung racket. — *Allie Ritzenberg, tennis player.*

1741 Talent is not just in hitting the ball. Talent also has to do with driving yourself to develop. I am tired of hearing about these players who look terrific hitting the ball, and how talented they are and how wonderful they could have been if they had bothered to use their talent. Part of talent is bothering. — *Nikki Pilic, tennis player.*

1742 Tennis doesn't need brashness or bad manners. The sport's bigger than any individual. — *Roy Emerson, tennis player, on hot-tempered players.*

1743 There are two types of players who cause a commotion: One guy gets angry at a linesman and reacts to what he thinks is a bad call and tries to change it; the other uses a situation or creates a problem to throw his opponent off in a conniving way. — *Gene Mayer, tennis player.*

1744 There is nothing like a great men's match. But to most people who are not on top of their game, it is more interesting to watch women's tennis because there is more rallying and you can actually see the strokes. — *Gladys Heldman, editor of World Tennis.*

1745 This isn't like going to see an old-timers' game in baseball where you say, "It's nice to see they're still alive." These guys are much more than alive. — *Bud Collins, announcer, on 45 year and above Grand Master tournaments.*

1746 Too long a tennis career can harden a girl. — *Chris Evert, tennis player.*

1747 We are all going to die, rich or poor, and I prefer to die in good health. — *Beppe Merlo, tennis player, on why he quit an investment job to play tennis.*

1748 We expend the same amount of energy as the men. We practice as much. We play just as hard. We contribute our share to the success of a tournament. — *Rosie Casals, tennis player, on the disparity in prize money between men and women.*

1749 We should encourage fans to scream or boo if they like, just like in baseball and football. This sport has too much stuffiness and protocol. It needs more pizzazz. — *Billie Jean King, tennis player.*

1750 What you see from a window is not always what is happening inside. — *Ion Tiriac, tennis player, on his reputation as a malcontent.*

1751 When I was in junior tennis, they called me a punk. Now I'm colorful. You know what the difference is? Colorful guys win. — *Vitas Gerulaitis, tennis player.*

1752 When you lose matches, you're more human. — *Chris Evert, tennis player.*

1753 When you walk around Wimbledon, you somehow get the feeling that it's going to be there 100 years from now. This place, they'll tear it down in 50 years and build another one. — *Arthur Ashe, tennis player, on the U.S. Open courts at Flushing Meadow.*

1754 Wimbledon is the great event. — *Rod Laver, tennis player.*

1755 With its organization, and its tradition of good manners and fair play, Wimbledon is unique in the world. — *Jean Borotra, 70-year-old former Wimbledon competitor.*

1756 You can almost watch a couple play mixed doubles and know whether they should stay together. — *Dr. Herbert Hendin, Columbia University psychiatrist.*

1757 You don't play people. You play a ball. You don't ever hit a guy in the butt and knock him over the net unless you're really upset. — *Vic Braden, tennis instructor.*

1758 You know what I once thought? I just thought, "What would tennis be like without me? And how could Wimbledon be going on if I wasn't there?" And then the time came when Wimbledon was going on pretty well and I wasn't there. I don't think anyone is missed and it doesn't matter whether it's sport or life. — *Helen Wills Moody, 70-year-old former Wimbledon champion.*

Track & Field

1759 Deliver me from the guys who think; just give me the ones who can run. — *Bob Giegengack, Yale track coach.*

1760 If a man coaches himself, then he has only himself to blame when he is beaten. — *Roger Bannister, miler.*

1761   If the kid's good enough, there are always ways of overcoming these little obstacles. — *Ted Banks, Texas of El Paso track coach, on a foreign prospect who spoke almost no English.*

1762   Italian men and Russian women never shave before a meet. — *Eddy Ottoz, Italian hurdler, on why he competes with a beard.*

1763   Man, they're not shades, they're my re-entry shields. — *Charlie Green, Nebraska sprinter, asked why he wears sunglasses at night meets.*

1764   The man who can drive himself further, once the effort gets painful, is the man who will win. — *Roger Bannister, miler.*

1765   Old shotputters never die, they just get weak. — *Otis Chander.*

1766   The only way we could make it would be if Jay Silvester and I threw at each other until one of us got hit. Then maybe we'd draw 10 people. — *Al Oerter, discus thrower, on professional track.*

1767   Politics say they must maintain a friendly relationship. But all the athletes know they are not friends, not friends at all. — *Daniel Korica, Yugoslav track coach, on the USSR-East German rivalry.*

1768   Relaxation is the key to running. — *Steve Prefontaine, middle distance runner.*

1769   This city must be designed as a testing ground for all us people who are destined to go to hell. — *Freddie Banks, track performer, on a meet in Bakersfield, California.*

1770   To say that politics is not a part of sports is not being realistic. When I run, I am more than a runner. I am a diplomat, an ambassador for my country.... The name of the nation is as much a part of competition as is my own name. Win or lose, the two are inseparable. — *Filbert Bayi, Tanzanian miler.*

1771   When God invented man, he wanted him to look like me. — *Brian Oldfield, shotputter.*

1772   With us, it's just a track meet. With them, it's war. — *Brutus Hamilton, U.S. track coach, on a duel meet with the Russians.*

Weightlifting & Bodybuilding

1773 The guy with the biggest butt lifts the biggest weights. — *Paul Anderson, U.S. weightlifting champion.*

1774 If somebody told weightlifters they could lift an extra five pounds by munching Brillo pads, there wouldn't be a clean pot within three miles of any gym in this country. — *Mark Cameron, weightlifter.*

1775 Most people walk around looking like pieces of junk. — *Mike Katz, body builder.*

1776 The weight cannot be feared. It must fear you. — *David Rigert, Russian weightlifter.*

Wrestling

1777 The goal of wrestling is to pin your man. I really don't see any purpose in buying wrestling mats if you're just going to stand on them. — *Port Robertson, Oklahoma wrestling coach.*

1778 I do not think I am gorgeous, but what is my opinion against millions of others. — *Gorgeous George, professional wrestler.*

Yachting (Americas Cup)

1779 Assuming no luck is involved in winning, the crew comes first, the sails next and the boat comes third and last. — *Philip Rhodes, Americas Cup defender in 1958.*

1780 The only difference between yachting writers and baseball writers is that yachting writers wear sneakers. — *Red Smith, writer, on covering the Americas Cup.*

1781 Watching an Americas Cup race is like watching grass grow. — *Ring Lardner, writer.*

1782 You do not win the Americas Cup. You defend it. — *Ted Turner, Americas Cup defender.*

Name Index

(Indexed here are utterers of quotations;
for persons as subjects, see Subject Index)

Aaron, Henry 223, 296, 471
Adamle, Mike 913
Adams, Franklin 407
Adams, Jack 1418
Adler, Zsigmond 771
Agase, Alex 1032, 1210
Agnew, Spiro 1578
Alexander, Grover Cleveland 441
Ali, Muhammad 696, 717, 732, 733, 734, 746, 752, 759, 764
Allen, Dick 167, 231, 278, 480
Allen, George 881, 888, 906, 908, 920, 981, 1005, 1145, 1215, 1248, 1268
Allen, Keith 1433, 1468
Allen, Mel 145
Alzado, Lyle 1603
Anderson, Bob 1554
Anderson, Paul 1773
Anderson, Sparky 65, 74, 299, 333, 373
Andreas, Bill 520
Andretti, Mario 2, 18, 21
Andujar, Joaquin 398
Aragon, Art 762
Arcaro, Eddie 1517, 1530, 1541, 1544, 1546, 1548
Archer, George 1301, 1333
Arias, Juan 1523
Arledge, Roone 1560, 1607
Arnsparger, Bill 1251
Ashburn, Richie 284
Ashe, Arthur 1587, 1703, 1709, 1731,

1753
Asimov, Isaac 1711
Aspin, Les 1586
Aspromonte, Bob 270
Aspromonte, Ken 84, 493
Atkins, Doug 1192
Attles, Al 687
Auerbach, Red 545, 550, 680
Autry, Gene 126
Averill, Earl 401
Awtrey, Dennis 629, 682

Backstrom, Ralph 1368
Baer, Bugs 139
Baiamonte, Philip 544
Bailey, Bob 390
Bailey, Sam 1171
Baker, Buddy 35
Baker, Sam 874
Balding, Al 1359
Ballard, Harold 1366, 1415, 1485
Balogh, Harry 778
Banks, Ernie 289, 488
Banks, Freddie 1769
Banks, Ted 1761
Bannister, Roger 1760, 1764
Barber, Bill 1432
Barber, Miller 1302
Barber, Red 371
Barzun, Jacques 459
Basilio, Carmen 755

147

Subject Index